Economics
for the Office

Economics for the Office

A Practical Introduction to Economics for Your Job or Business

Susan Krug Friedman

Susan Krug Friedman Reports
Bloomington, Indiana

Library of Congress Catalog Card Number 93-70086

ISBN 0-9635628-1-9

Printed in the United States of America

Published by Susan Krug Friedman Reports,
P.O. Box 5803, Bloomington, Indiana 47407-5803

The data presented in this report are meant to be representative and are in many cases subject to revision by the issuing organizations. The reader should contact these organizations, the latest editions of the sources cited, or other original data sources for updated information.

The author assumes no responsibility or liability resulting from the use of the information presented herein or from possible errors or omissions. The author makes no representation as to the accuracy of the material obtained from sources cited.

For financial, accounting, and legal matters, contractual and other agreements, the reader should seek appropriate professional services.

For Edward

Contents

              The Economic Picture: GDP and
                  Business Cycles
              Employment: U.S.
              Employment: Regions

              A Look at Regional Data
              Industry Measures

Contents

Contents

Figures and Tables

Figures

Tables

Figures and Tables

Acknowledgments

In writing this book, I would like to acknowledge the support of many individuals. I am fortunate to have numerous role models: my teachers, former colleagues and supervisors, and my friends and family.

My grandparents Theise and Krug and my parents continue to be an inspiration, for their ability to meet challenges with enthusiasm and for their appreciation of the limitless potential of the U.S. To my mother, Hilde T. Krug, and to my late father, Harry H. Krug, I owe a special debt of gratitude for their love and dedication. They spared no effort for my education and set the example for a lifetime of learning. My brother, John L. Krug, helped steer me towards economics as an undergraduate. His well-reasoned judgment and open-mindedness exemplify the attitude that objective analysis requires, and his empathetic good humor provides the needed equilibrium. I would also like to thank my parents-in-law, Sara S. Friedman and the late Joseph H. Friedman, for their kindness and support.

I would not have been able to undertake this publishing project without the confidence placed in me by my husband, Edward H. Friedman. In addition to giving guidance and encouragement, he provides me with a model for scholarship and commitment to goals, however quixotic.

My sincere thanks go to Werner Sichel, for his perceptive comments and constructive suggestions on an early draft of this book. I am also indebted to David B. Jones for his careful review and valuable thoughts. I would like to thank Marshall J. Vest for reading several portions of the text and for his very helpful observations. The comments and scholarly insights of Thomas M. Humphrey are also much appreciated. I am thankful for the consideration of all of these gracious and accomplished individuals.

Finally, I would like to acknowledge the efforts of some people without whom this book or today's economics profession would not be possible: the individuals in federal and state offices who compile and analyze the statistics that are the foundation of economic work. My special thanks go to these dedicated and often overlooked professionals.

Introduction

This book reflects my experience of more than fifteen years as a business economist. It is intended to serve as an "in-house" consultant to you, to give you some tips on using economics to do your job or to run your business more effectively.

The topics covered in the following chapters relate to the concerns of individuals at work: marketing, managing staff and resources, planning and budgeting, accounting, developing and auditing contracts, purchasing, inventory control, credit policies, public and customer relations, and advertising. These are all essential functions whether you are in business for yourself or work for someone else.

The discussion assumes no previous knowledge of economics or business theory. I have written the text with the hope that it will be useful and interesting to individuals with no formal training in economics. It is also intended to be helpful to those of you who have studied economics and would like some examples of practical applications of your knowledge to the business world, as well as references to valuable source materials.

Chapters One and Two introduce some key sources of information on markets and related data classification systems. Inflation—measurement and analysis—is the topic of Chapters Three and Four. Chapter Five presents some important financial concepts relating to the valuation of money with respect to time, interest rates, and inflation. Business forecasting is the subject of Chapter Six. Chapter Seven gives examples of how economics can be used for business analysis and management and provides some concluding principles. "A Note to Nonprofit Organizations" follows Chapter Seven. The reader will also find an appendix, which lists economic resources according to the chapters in which they are referenced, and a topical index.

One of the challenges in writing this book was selecting which economic indicators and concepts to discuss. The abundance of information on the U.S. economy is inspiring—and at times overwhelming. I have tried to pick those areas that are of practical concern and interest to individuals in their jobs. The footnotes and appendix provide references to readers who would like to pursue these topics further.

Tracking our economic system is a dynamic process. The reader should note that economic data—and sometimes data classifications—are subject to revision and that updated sources should be consulted when incorporating statistics into a project.

Economics is a powerful tool, both from an informational and an analytical standpoint. I hope that this brief book will be helpful to you, in understanding some major concepts and resources and how they can relate to your own work.

Chapter One

Economics and Your Markets: Part One

Your job—no matter what it is—depends on your market. Whether you work for (or own) a company that manufactures a product or provides a service, customers determine the viability of your job. If you work in a large organization, your immediate "customers" may be fellow employees (your boss or people in another department), but no one is insulated from the market. Without customers, there is no need for your business, regardless of how well you— and your department or company—may be doing your job.

The Economic Picture: GDP and Business Cycles

To assess the market for your business, you first need to evaluate the overall economic climate at any particular point in time. Just as many kinds of industries and enterprises make up the U.S. economy, the total economy provides the foundation on which individual businesses depend. There is a galaxy of information on the U.S. economy, but just a few key indicators, a number of which will be highlighted in this and the following chapter, can signal the general state of national business conditions.

Gross domestic product (GDP) is a broad-based measure of the market value of output and includes both the goods and the services that are produced in the U.S. (by labor and property situated here).[1] **Real** gross domestic product is gross domestic product adjusted for inflation and is measured in constant dollars.

That is, real gross domestic product shows what the value of U.S. output would be if there were no inflation. Real GDP gives a picture of what is actually happening, without the distortion of price level changes. This is analogous to comparing your income now (current income) with your income ten years ago in terms of actual purchasing power. (Chapter Two discusses how to adjust for inflation.)

Data on real gross domestic product are reported by newspapers and other media nationwide. The figures themselves are prepared by the federal government: GDP is calculated for each calendar quarter by the U.S. Department of Commerce, Bureau of Economic Analysis. The statistics (which are subject to a revision schedule) are published in sources such as the *Survey of Current Business*. (Please see the appendix for information on cited publications and related resources.)

Figure 1.1
Real Gross Domestic Product, U.S.
1960-91, Annual Data

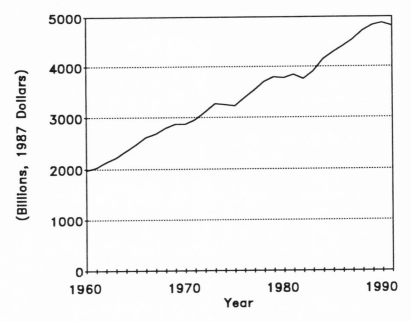

Note: Data are subject to revision. Consult the *Survey of Current Business* for printed updates or the U.S. Department of Commerce, Bureau of Economic Analysis, for the most current data.

Source: U.S. Department of Commerce, Economics and Statistics Administration, Bureau of Economic Analysis, *Survey of Current Business*, February 1992, p. 32, and July 1992, p. 49.

Previously, the Bureau of Economic Analysis focused on gross national product (GNP) as the major indicator of U.S. output. GNP is still an important concept and is reported with national income and product data. GNP measures output from property and labor, regardless of location, provided by residents of the U.S.

Figure 1.1 on page 5 gives you a perspective on real GDP over time. The graph is actually a capsule history of the U.S. economy.

Three trends are evident in the figure. First, the overwhelming direction of the U.S. economy has been positive. Growth, shown by the increasing values, has been significant. Second, there is a definite cyclical pattern, with periods of growth interrupted by downturns. For a listing of business cycles since the mid-19th century, see data from the National Bureau of Economic Research, Inc., published in the *Survey of Current Business*.[2] You will find information on all business cycles during the period, their length and their occurrence relative to times of war or peace. The data make it clear that upswings and downturns have consistently characterized the U.S. economy.

The third trend apparent in the data is that the pace of

Figure 1.2

Increase in Real GDP
Overall Percent Change

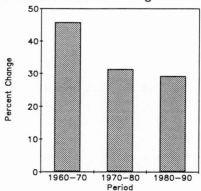

Note: Percentage changes are based on data in Figure 1.1.

growth, as shown by the percentage changes, has decreased in recent decades relative to the 1960s. This trend is illustrated in Figure 1.2.

Employment: U.S.

Employment, another major economic indicator, displays similar trends: a clear upward direction, intermittent decreases, and slightly slower percentage gains over time. Figure 1.3 shows data for employment on nonfarm payrolls,

Figure 1.3
Employment Trend, U.S., 1960-91
Number of Employees on Nonagricultural Payrolls

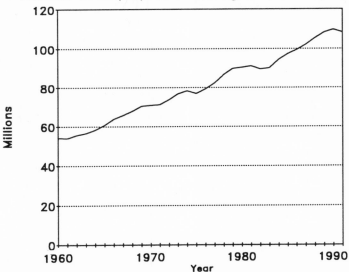

Note: Data are subject to revision. Consult recent issues of *Employment and Earnings* for updates.
Source: U.S. Department of Labor, Bureau of Labor Statistics, *Employment and Earnings*, July 1992, p. 81.

as published by the U.S. Department of Labor, Bureau of Labor Statistics. As of 1991, real GDP was close to two-and-a-half times and employment was about twice the levels in 1960. These figures demonstrate the long-term vigor and the tremendous growth that have characterized the U.S. economy over the years.

Note that with any kind of trend analysis, you need to be aware of the time period covered. Of particular concern are the starting and ending choices. Consider the hypothetical data shown in Figure 1.4. If the time span begins at one of the low points of a set of data (such as year 12 in this example), when business activity has fallen from the previous period, the subsequent percentage changes will be higher than if calculated based on an earlier year (such as year 7, shown on the dotted line) as a starting point.

Figure 1.4
Trends over Time
(Hypothetical Data)

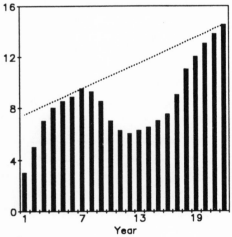

The increase in employment in Figure 1.3 is 17.5 percent between 1975 and 1980. It is only 15.5 percent between 1974 and 1980, even though this covers a longer period, since there was a drop in 1975. For this reason, you should look at more than just the statistics for the starting and ending years or the percentage change between those years. There may also be fluctuations during intervening years that are masked by the overall percentage changes.

Employment: Regions

If your customers are defined by a geographic region, there are several important economic statistics you should evaluate. Employment data are available for every state and for many subdivisions of states, such as metropolitan areas. These statistics will tell you how many people have jobs in a particular place and will allow you to make comparisons over time.

The data will also give you information as to the types of jobs individuals hold and on the unemployment rate, which measures the share of the labor force that is unemployed. Note that the labor force includes people who are seeking work as well as those who are working.[3]

The material in Table 1.1 is based on information at the state level available from *Employment and Earnings*, a monthly journal, and the *Handbook of Labor Statistics*, both produced by the Bureau of Labor Statistics of the U.S. Department of Labor. In addition to data for all the states, *Employment and Earnings* has information for many metropolitan communities. You can find these reports in the government publications or reference sections of many large libraries or order them directly from the government.[4]

Table 1.1 exposes several important points. First, the states vary in their pace of growth over time. Reflecting the national economy, many states had higher percentage gains in employment in the 1970s than in the 1980s. Patterns of growth have also differed among the states. Compare, for example, Arizona's growth percentage in the 1970s with that of other areas.

It is also true that the overall percentage changes over the decades do not tell the whole story. Between 1970 and

Table 1.1
Employment Trends for Selected States

	Percentage Change in the Number of Nonfarm Employees*		Years when Employment Dropped from Previous Year*
State	**1970-80**	**1980-90**	**1970-91**
Arizona	85.2	46.5	1975,1982
California	41.8	30.3	1971,1982,1991
Kansas	39.2	15.2	1970,1971,1980,1982
Mass.	18.2	12.3	1970,1971,1975,1982, 1989,1990,1991
Michigan	14.8	15.3	1970,1971,1974,1975, 1980,1981,1982,1991
North Carolina	33.5	31.0	1975,1982,1991
Oregon	47.0	19.8	1975,1980,1981,1982, 1991
Penn.	9.2	8.8	1970,1971,1975,1980 1981,1982,1983,1991
Tenn.	31.6	25.5	1975,1980,1982,1991
Texas	61.4	21.4	1983,1986,1987
Utah	54.3	31.4	None

*As measured by the number of employees on nonagricultural payrolls.

Table 1.1 (continued)

Note: Data are subject to revision.

Source: U.S. Department of Labor, Bureau of Labor Statistics, *Employment and Earnings*, May 1992, pp. 132-49; May 1991, pp. 124-39; May 1990, pp. 128-43, and *Handbook of Labor Statistics*, August 1989, Bulletin 2340, pp. 323-25.

1990, employment in the states in Table 1.1 showed substantial net gains. During this same period, however, there were several times when employment dropped in numerous places. As you can see from Table 1.1, certain economic downturns have been difficult to avoid, with employment slipping in many parts of the country at the same time.

Some states have clearly been more vigorous than others, and some states have—at least in the past—been able to weather the ups and downs of the national economy relatively well in terms of employment. (Note that Table 1.1 does not indicate how severe the declines were, only that they did occur to some extent.) These are certainly important considerations for businesses deciding where to locate operations and where to focus their marketing activities.

Percentage changes, as shown in Table 1.1, allow you to make comparisons among areas that are very different in size. The percentages do not tell you what the absolute gain or loss is over time, however. Consequently, you also need to look at the magnitude of these markets. A large state may have had only a moderate percentage gain in jobs, but that may represent a much greater absolute increase than that experienced by a smaller state.[5]

For example, between 1980 and 1990, employment on nonagricultural payrolls grew by about 31 percent in Utah. In California, the percentage gain was approximately 30 percent. The absolute increase in these employment figures was about 173,000 in Utah and about 3 million in California. Thus, all three factors—growth, balance, and size—are key economic considerations.

Summary

The more you know about your markets, the better prepared you will be to evaluate the sales potential of your business. Your own markets, in turn, relate to the overall economy. Two major indicators, real gross domestic product and employment, can give you a picture of the general state of the economy, relative to recent and longer-term history. Has the record shown declines, stagnation, or growth? This information will help to give you a broad perspective on the environment for your business and a foundation for the diverse market-related economic resources explored in Chapter Two.

Notes

1. Gross domestic product is comprised of personal consumption expenditures, gross private domestic investment, government purchases, and net exports (exports minus imports). For the breakdown of these major categories, see the U.S. Department of Commerce, Bureau of Economic Analysis, *Survey of Current Business* (monthly). Data on Gross National Product (GNP) and real GNP are also reported in the *Survey of Current Business.*

2. U.S. Department of Commerce, Bureau of Economic Analysis, *Survey of Current Business.* A listing appears in the October 1992 issue, p. C-45. Check for more recent information that may have been published subsequently.

3. If available for employment, individuals who are waiting to be called back to jobs or who, within 30 days, will be starting a new job do not have to be seeking work to be included in the labor force (with the unemployed segment). Source: *Employment and Earnings,* August 1990, pp. 119-20, and U.S. Department of Commerce, Bureau of the Census, *Statistical Abstract of the United States,* 1990, p. 376. The labor force includes "employed" and "unemployed" individuals, as specifically defined in the government data. Activities such as doing one's own housekeeping, for example, do not qualify an individual as "employed." For definitions of specific concepts, see the explanatory material in *Employment and Earnings,* published monthly by the U.S. Department of Labor, Bureau of Labor Statistics.

4. U.S. Department of Labor, Bureau of Labor Statistics, *Employment and Earnings,* monthly, and *Handbook of Labor Statistics.*

5. This is also true when looking at trends for a single growing economy, such as the U.S., over time. A given percentage increase in jobs represents more new positions as the economy gains in total size.

Chapter Two

Economics and Your Markets: Part Two

In Chapter One, we discussed several key output and employment indicators. These measures give you a perspective on the overall status of the economy, and they enable you to answer some fundamental questions. Has economic output been rising? Have more people been employed? This chapter provides you with some further guides to assessing national and regional economies, to help you in collecting and interpreting information from which you can start to construct your own business analysis and strategies.

Along with gross domestic product and employment, income is a valuable gauge of economic strength. The Bureau of Economic Analysis at the U.S. Department of Commerce is a top source of information on income. National income and personal income data are published in the *Survey of Current Business*.

A Look at Regional Data

The Bureau of Economic Analysis also compiles extensive data on state and local personal income (including per-capita income) through its Regional Economic Measurement Division. Data for the states and for localities (i.e., counties and metropolitan areas) are published in the *Survey of Current Business*.[1]

In these reports, you will find a wealth of information for the U.S. as a whole and for each state. Extensive industry information allows you to see the sources of income and to make comparisons among activities in various regions of the country. Through the earnings data, you can determine, for example, how much the retail trade or health services industries contribute to different states' economies, or the relative impact of the construction or communications industries. You can compare these findings among states or regions (i.e., New England) or to national averages.[2]

The Bureau of the Census, another branch of the U.S. Department of Commerce, compiles construction data by area. The *Current Construction Reports* have extensive information on building activity. Statistics are published on indicators such as building permits and on actual housing starts. In one monthly report, "Housing Units Authorized by Building Permits," for example, you will find information for a large number of locations across the U.S.[3]

The *Statistical Abstract of the United States* has an excellent reference section on sources by topics.[4] You can find the names and publishers of data on a wide range of subjects that may be relevant to your markets, such as communications, consumer income and spending, food, health, and money and banking. The *Statistical Abstract* also includes listings of statistical abstracts for the states and the organizations that publish them. The *Statistical Abstract* is produced annually by the U.S. Department of Commerce, Bureau of the Census, and is widely available in libraries.[5]

The Federal Reserve System is another valuable data source. As our central bank, the Federal Reserve Board of Governors and the district Federal Reserve Banks monitor business conditions nationally and regionally. A list of district Federal Reserve Banks is included in the appendix.

The Federal Reserve Bank of Philadelphia produces a report listing work published by the Research Departments of the Federal Reserve. This index, called the *Fed in Print,* is a very helpful guide to information. The index includes references to an assortment of regional economic indicators published by the various Federal Reserve Research Departments, which may relate directly to business conditions in your markets.[6] Private financial institutions, such as large banks, also monitor local business conditions and may produce reports of interest to you. These reports are often distributed by economics or public affairs departments.

The federal government provides a useful classification scheme that relates to geographic areas. The U.S. Office of Management and Budget defines metropolitan statistical areas (MSAs). There are also primary (PMSA) and consolidated metropolitan statistical area (CMSA) classifications. A description (and listing) of metropolitan areas is in the *Statistical Abstract of the United States.*[7]

For New England, there are also New England County Metropolitan Areas (NECMAs). These additional classifications are made since New England MSAs are based on towns and cities instead of counties.[8]

The definitions of metropolitan areas such as MSAs are subject to change, as a reflection of changes in population. Over time, the definitions of MSAs cover an increasing share of the population of the U.S.[9]

Industry Measures

What if your market is an industry rather than a geographical area? Here, too, employment data may be very useful. *Employment and Earnings* has detailed employment data by type of industry, according to categories under the Standard Industrial Classification or SIC code system. Perhaps you want to sell supplies to be used in beauty shops or aprons to be used in restaurants. Have these been growth markets? The information in *Employment and Earnings* shows you what recent employment trends have been for beauty shops and for "eating and drinking places," as well as for an extensive variety of other establishments, such as car dealers, furniture manufacturers, and hospitals.[10]

The Board of Governors of the Federal Reserve System compiles indexes of industrial production. These measures of output are available on a monthly basis in *The Federal*

Reserve Bulletin. The indexes give you a perspective over time on production by different kinds of industries and in various markets. For example, you can track the trends in production activity in the consumer goods market—or in an industry such as apparel products or printing and publishing.[11] Indicators such as these are important barometers of market trends, providing insights to companies whose sales may depend on other types of businesses as well as on final consumers.

In addition to the well-known U.S. censuses that are undertaken for population and housing every ten years, there are economic censuses. These reports contain very useful business data. The economic censuses are carried out every five years and include the following: Census of Construction Industries, Census of Manufactures, Census of Mineral Industries, Census of Service Industries, Census of Retail Trade, Census of Wholesale Trade, and Census of Transportation. (There are also some other associated reports.) Although separate from the economic censuses, there are additional censuses for agriculture and governments.[12]

Information in the censuses is collected for the U.S. and for various geographical divisions, such as states and metropolitan statistical areas (MSAs). Some statistics are even compiled by zip code. Data vary by type of census, but generally include the number of firms and establishments, employment, sales or value of work or shipments, various operating expenses, and payroll (with a range in the items, level of detail, and geographical categories that may be available).[13] This information can be very helpful in assessing how your firm has done relative to the industry and in analyzing market opportunities. Reports are printed or available in computer formats.[14]

A large amount of Census and other government data is organized according to the Standard Industrial Classification or SIC system, mentioned earlier in this section. These categories are determined by the U.S. Office of Management and Budget and were revised in 1987. Establishments (such as a store or factory) are categorized into major industry divisions: Agriculture, Forestry and Fishing; Mining; Construction; Manufacturing; Transportation, Communications, Electric, Gas, and Sanitary Services; Wholesale Trade; Retail Trade; Finance, Insurance, and Real Estate; Services; Public Administration; and Nonclassifiable Establishments. These headings are then divided into two-digit, three-digit, and four-digit categories, with increasing levels of detail.[15]

Table 2.1 provides some examples from the Standard Industrial Classification system. As you can see, these classifications allow you to focus on specific activities. Information at these levels can be extremely useful in studying your competition or potential markets.

You can find a treasure of information on employment, payroll, and establishments by SIC code in *County Business Patterns*. The studies, published by the U.S. Bureau of the Census, give an in-depth profile of states and counties by industry.

In addition to industry codes, there are approximately 11,000 manufacturing product codes, with seven digits, in the Census of Manufactures. The product codes are organized into product classes, which have five digits. For example, under the five-digit code for "Jewelry, made of platinum metals and karat gold" (39111), you can find "Fraternal, college, and school rings" (39111 11) and "Wedding rings"(39111 12). The 1987 Census of Manufactures shows information such as the number of companies (with at least $100,000 in shipments) and the dollar value of

Table 2.1
Examples of SIC Codes

Division: Services	
Example of a Major Group: 73	Business Services
Industry Group No. 731	Advertising
Industry No. 7311	Advertising Agencies
7312	Outdoor Advertising Services
7313	Radio, Television, and Publishers' Advertising Representatives
7319	Advertising, not elsewhere classified

Division: Retail Trade	
Example of a Major Group: 57	Home Furniture, Furnishings, and Equipment Stores
Industry Group No. 571	Home Furniture and Furnishings Stores
Industry No. 5712	Furniture Stores
5713	Floor Covering Stores
5714	Drapery, Curtain, and Upholstery Stores
5719	Misc. Homefurnishings Stores

Source: Executive Office of the President, Office of Management and Budget, *Standard Industrial Classification Manual*, 1987, pp. 360-61 and 325-26.

21

shipments for these seven-digit product classifications, according to data available in 1987 and 1982.[16]

Some additional classification systems are also used in the economic censuses. These are explained in the censuses and in a helpful report entitled *Guide to the 1987 Economic Censuses and Related Statistics.*[17]

Other Markets

Government data can provide help if your market is defined as a segment—such as an age group—of the national population. The U.S. Census is the premier source of population information. The *Statistical Abstract of the United States,* discussed earlier in this chapter, is a handy reference for population data as well as for a myriad of economic statistics.

For further information, you can explore other government reports, such as the *County and City Data Book* (U.S. Bureau of the Census), and the work of the many private agencies that publish studies of markets and industries. Some sources may be available in computer formats. The reference staff at your local library can help guide you to reports and directories of such information. I have emphasized government reports because they are wonderful sources of data—and are accessible at minimal expense to you.

Measuring Market Strength

Your markets have several dimensions, including product and location. In addition to considering the overall
economic picture, as described in Chapter One, you need to
evaluate the vigor of the areas in which you do business.

How can you measure the strength of your market?
Growth—vitality—is an overriding objective from a sales
standpoint. In a competitive economy, you want to pick a
market that is increasing, offering rising potential.[18]

From a financial perspective, you—and the people who
may be lending you or your company money—also want a
market mix that is balanced. Diversification (that is carefully
done) is important. You do not want to be heavily dependent
on one type of customer who, in turn, may be highly
dependent on one industry. A community with only one very
large employer, for example, is a less attractive market than
an area with several different kinds of businesses. (Chapter
Seven offers some further perspectives on diversification.)

The resources discussed in this chapter help to provide
the kinds of information you need in order to answer crucial
marketing questions. How large is the market? Has the
market been growing? Has the number of potential customers
been shrinking or increasing over time, or has the total
remained the same? How smooth is the market trend? Has
it been steadily rising, or are there significant variations from
year to year? A more complete market study also requires an
evaluation of your competition and a look at future trends
(discussed in Chapter Six), but gathering basic economic
information is the essential first step.

Summary

There are numerous information sources, many of which are provided by the federal government, that can help you to understand the economics of your customer markets. Statistics on indicators such as income or construction activity, for example, are produced by the U.S. Department of Commerce.

Several classification systems are used for government data. These include definitions for metropolitan areas, such as metropolitan statistical areas (MSAs), and the Standard Industrial Classification (SIC) system.

The U.S. Bureau of the Census of the U.S. Department of Commerce prepares economic as well as population censuses. The U.S. Department of Labor also compiles information related to the nation's industries, as reflected in earnings and job data.

The Federal Reserve System provides indexes of industrial production and publishes other economic information. In addition, a number of private financial institutions and both state and private research organizations publish economic reports and special market and industry studies. All of these resources can help you to assess the size, diversity, and growth characteristics of your market.

Notes

1. See, for example, the *Survey of Current Business*, August 1992, and April 1992. An excellent description of information available from the Bureau of Economic Analysis is in the February 1992 issue of the *Survey of Current Business*, pp. 37-58. The article is entitled "User's Guide to BEA Information."

2. See, for example, "The Comprehensive Revision of State Personal Income," by the Regional Economic Measurement Division, in *Survey of Current Business*, August 1992, pp. 44-59.

3. U.S. Department of Commerce, Bureau of the Census, Current Construction Reports, C40, *Housing Units Authorized by Building Permits*. Other sources for housing data are listed in U.S. Bureau of the Census, *Statistical Abstract of the United States: 1991*, 111th edition (Washington, D.C.: 1991), pp. 869-70.

4. *Statistical Abstract of the United States: 1991*, Appendix 1.

5. The *Statistical Abstract* can also be purchased from the Superintendent of Documents, U.S. Government Printing Office, Washington, D.C. 20402.

6. The *Fed in Print* is available from the Federal Reserve Bank of Philadelphia, Research Department, 4th Floor, Publications Desk, 10 Independence Mall, Philadelphia, Pennsylvania 19106.

7. *Statistical Abstract of the United States: 1991*, pp. 904-12.

8. *Ibid.*, p. 905.

9. *Ibid.*, pp. 27, 905.

10. U.S. Department of Labor, Bureau of Labor Statistics, *Employment and Earnings*, monthly.

11. Board of Governors of the Federal Reserve System, *Federal Reserve Bulletin,* January 1992, pp. A47-A48.

12. U.S. Department of Commerce, Bureau of the Census, *Guide to the Economic Censuses and Related Statistics,* EC 87-R-2, January 1990, p. 1.

13. *Ibid.*, p. 3.

14. For Census information, contact your local library or write to Customer Services, Bureau of the Census, Washington, D.C. 20233.

15. Executive Office of the President, Office of Management and Budget, *Standard Industrial Classification Manual,* 1987, p. 12.

16. The four-digit industry code is 3911 for "Jewelry, Precious Metal." U.S. Department of Commerce, Bureau of the Census, *1987 Census of Manufactures*, MC87-1-39A, Industry Series, "Jewelry, Silverware, and Plated Ware," pp. VII, 39A-11, A-3.

17. U.S. Department of Commerce, Bureau of the Census, *Guide to the 1987 Economic Censuses and Related Statistics,* EC87-R-2, January 1990, pp. 7-10.

18. A stable—or even declining—market can also present rising sales potential, if the likelihood of competition is low and you are able to gain an increasing share of the market.

Chapter Three

Inflation and Your Business: Part One

Whatever your job or profession, you have to deal with inflation in today's economy. Increases in the overall level of prices affect the costs of doing business, what you (or your employer) charge for the goods and services you provide, and what it costs for you, your customers, employees in general, and retirees to run a household.

How is Inflation Measured?

In 1950, you could buy a pair of women's dress shoes for $5 and a high-quality men's suit for $55. Compare those figures with today's prices! On the other hand, an 18-inch portable color television set sold for about $370 in 1970. In 1992, you could buy a higher quality 19-inch model for under $220.

We can make comparisons like these through old newspaper ads (as I did) or even with data that we might collect ourselves. Fortunately, more systematic and efficient methods of following price changes over time are available, thanks to the research of the federal government and other organizations.

There are several ways to measure inflation. One popular method is to use the Consumer Price Index. The Consumer Price Index is based on the prices of goods and services needed by urban consumer households. The measure is called an index because it shows changes over time relative to a base, rather than actual costs in dollars and cents. The goods and services are assumed to be basically constant over time, so that just the average variation in prices of a set "market basket" are tracked.[1]

The Consumer Price Index for January 1992 was 138.1 using the index value for "All Urban Consumers." This is a broad-based consumer measure. There is also an index for "Urban Wage Earners and Clerical Workers," which is more narrow in scope. The base period for the index is 1982-84, such that 1982-84 = 100.[2] This means that as of January 1992, it took $138.10 to buy what $100.00 would have bought in 1982-84. The 1982-84 base period reflects Consumer Expenditure Surveys undertaken during those years.[3]

Over time, the base periods of the Consumer Price Index are updated. Before the latest change, the base period was 1967,[4] and you can still find data expressed in that base period in publications such as the *Monthly Labor Review,* produced by the U.S. Department of Labor, Bureau of Labor Statistics.

Consider some other examples. Table 3.1 provides monthly figures for the Consumer Price Index, All Urban Consumers, for 1980 through 1992.

Table 3.1
The Consumer Price Index
All Urban Consumers, Monthly Data
U.S. City Average
(1982-84 = 100)

Month	1980	1981	1982	1983
Jan.	77.8	87.0	94.3	97.8
Feb.	78.9	87.9	94.6	97.9
March	80.1	88.5	94.5	97.9
April	81.0	89.1	94.9	98.6
May	81.8	89.8	95.8	99.2
June	82.7	90.6	97.0	99.5
July	82.7	91.6	97.5	99.9
August	83.3	92.3	97.7	100.2
Sept.	84.0	93.2	97.9	100.7
Oct.	84.8	93.4	98.2	101.0
Nov.	85.5	93.7	98.0	101.2
Dec.	86.3	94.0	97.6	101.3

Table 3.1 (continued)

Month	1984	1985	1986	1987
Jan.	101.9	105.5	109.6	111.2
Feb.	102.4	106.0	109.3	111.6
March	102.6	106.4	108.8	112.1
April	103.1	106.9	108.6	112.7
May	103.4	107.3	108.9	113.1
June	103.7	107.6	109.5	113.5
July	104.1	107.8	109.5	113.8
August	104.5	108.0	109.7	114.4
Sept.	105.0	108.3	110.2	115.0
Oct.	105.3	108.7	110.3	115.3
Nov.	105.3	109.0	110.4	115.4
Dec.	105.3	109.3	110.5	115.4

Note: The Bureau of Labor Statistics modified the homeownership cost component of the CPI, All Urban Consumers, in 1983. The CPI was revised effective as of the release of data for January 1987 (*Monthly Labor Review*, August 1990, p. 57). In 1988, the reference base was changed to 1982-84=100 (Bureau of Labor Statistics News,"The Consumer Price Index--January 1988").

Table 3.1 (continued)

Month	1988	1989	1990	1991	1992
Jan.	115.7	121.1	127.4	134.6	138.1
Feb.	116.0	121.6	128.0	134.8	138.6
March	116.5	122.3	128.7	135.0	139.3
April	117.1	123.1	128.9	135.2	139.5
May	117.5	123.8	129.2	135.6	139.7
June	118.0	124.1	129.9	136.0	140.2
July	118.5	124.4	130.4	136.2	140.5
August	119.0	124.6	131.6	136.6	140.9
Sept.	119.8	125.0	132.7	137.2	141.3
Oct.	120.2	125.6	133.5	137.4	141.8
Nov.	120.3	125.9	133.8	137.8	142.0
Dec.	120.5	126.1	133.8	137.9	141.9

Source: U.S. Department of Labor, Bureau of Labor Statistics; without seasonal adjustment.

How much did prices paid by consumers increase between June 1980 and June 1990? This can be determined by taking the percentage change between the index values for the two dates:

Value for June 1990 - Value for June 1980
Value for June 1980

$$= \frac{129.9 - 82.7}{82.7}$$

$$= .571 \text{ or } 57.1\%$$

In a similar way, you can determine the percentage increase between selected years. Table 3.2 shows annual averages for the Consumer Price Index, All Urban Consumers, from 1960 to 1992. Rather than simply looking at December-to-December percentage changes, you can look at changes between the annual averages for two given years.

For example,

Average value for 1991-Average value for 1981
Average value for 1981

$$= \frac{136.2 - 90.9}{90.9}$$

$$= .498 \text{ or about 50 percent}$$

Note that to obtain the average annual values, you take the sum of the monthly figures for the year and divide by twelve.

Table 3.2
The Consumer Price Index
All Urban Consumers, Annual Averages
U.S. City Average (1982-84 = 100)

Year	Index, All Items	Percent Change (from Previous Year)	Year	Index, All Items	Percent Change (from Previous Year)
1960	29.6	1.7	1977	60.6	6.5
1961	29.9	1.0	1978	65.2	7.6
1962	30.2	1.0	1979	72.6	11.3
1963	30.6	1.3	1980	82.4	13.5
1964	31.0	1.3	1981	90.9	10.3
1965	31.5	1.6	1982	96.5	6.2
1966	32.4	2.9	1983	99.6	3.2
1967	33.4	3.1	1984	103.9	4.3
1968	34.8	4.2	1985	107.6	3.6
1969	36.7	5.5	1986	109.6	1.9
1970	38.8	5.7	1987	113.6	3.6
1971	40.5	4.4	1988	118.3	4.1
1972	41.8	3.2	1989	124.0	4.8
1973	44.4	6.2	1990	130.7	5.4
1974	49.3	11.0	1991	136.2	4.2
1975	53.8	9.1	1992	140.3	3.0
1976	56.9	5.8			

Note: Annual averages are obtained from monthly data. The market basket of products and services in the CPI has been revised over time. For example, there was an update in 1978 and one in 1987 (Charles Mason

Table 3.2 (continued)

and Clifford Butler, "New Basket of Goods and Services Being Priced in Revised CPI," *Monthly Labor Review*, January 1987, pp. 3-22.) See note from Table 3.1.

Source: U.S. Department of Labor, Bureau of Labor Statistics. Data are published in sources such as *Handbook of Labor Statistics*, August 1989, p. 475, the *Statistical Abstract of the United States* (e.g., 1990, pp. 468, 471), and the *Monthly Labor Review* (e.g., March 1992, p. 79, for 1983-91).

The U.S. Bureau of Labor Statistics reports monthly percentage changes for the Consumer Price Index before and after adjustments for seasonal variations. The seasonal adjustment means that the reported price changes are those that have occurred apart from the normal variations between different months of the year. For example, the prices of fresh fruits and vegetables have a typical seasonal pattern. (Note that seasonally adjusted CPIs are subject to revision; seasonal adjustment factors are recalculated by the Bureau of Labor Statistics.)[5]

Do prices in general ever decrease? The Consumer Price Index has fallen at times. Prices dropped significantly during the Great Depression. Between 1929 and 1933, the Consumer Price Index dropped by 24 percent.[6] In more recent years, declines in the overall price level in the economy have not been seen frequently, but they have occurred. In 1986, for example, consumer prices declined slightly in February, March, and April, as seen in Table 3.1 (which is without seasonal adjustment). You would calculate the price changes the same way as shown above:

Value for April 1986 - Value for Jan. 1986
Value for Jan. 1986

$$= \frac{108.6 - 109.6}{109.6}$$

$= -.009$ or $-.9\%$

How to Use Price Index Data

Suppose you earned $20,000 in 1980 and $32,000 in 1991. Did your income increase relative to inflation or in what is called "real" terms? First we can say that your dollar income increased by 60 percent, while we know that inflation over the period was

Average CPI for 1991 - Average CPI for 1980
Average CPI value for 1980

Using the data from Table 3.2 gives us

$$\frac{136.2 - 82.4}{82.4}$$

$= .653$ or 65.3%

Consequently, your earnings increased by somewhat less than the rate of inflation.

A more precise way to evaluate your earnings is to adjust them for inflation using the price index. The index value for 1980 is 82.4, and the value for 1991 is 136.2. The base is

35

1982-84 (which equals 100). In inflation-adjusted dollars, your 1991 income would be

$\dfrac{32,000}{136.2}$ x 100 = \$23,495 in 1982-84 base dollars,

and your 1980 income would be

$\dfrac{20,000}{82.4}$ x 100 = \$24,272 in 1982-84 base dollars.

By looking at the index numbers, we know that it only took \$82.40 in 1980 to buy the same items (as measured by the Consumer Price Index) that required \$100 in 1982-84 but that it took \$136.20 to buy them in 1991. Consequently, the \$20,000 you earned in 1980 had a higher purchasing power than an equivalent amount in 1991. In "constant" dollar terms, your \$20,000 income in 1980 was worth slightly more than your \$32,000 income in 1991.

To put income (or expenses) into inflation-adjusted dollars, take

$\dfrac{\text{Income in year "x"}}{\text{Index value for year "x"}}$ times 100

= Income in base-period dollars.

Here, the base period is 1982-84 (which equals 100).

What if you want to express all figures in terms of 1991 purchasing power? To do this, take

$$\frac{\text{Income in year "x"}}{\text{Index value for year "x"}} \text{ times (Index value for the year in which you want to express the dollars)}$$

$$\frac{32,000}{136.2} \times 136.2 = 32,000 = \text{1991 income expressed in 1991 dollars}$$

$$\frac{20,000}{82.4} \times 136.2 = 33,058 = \text{1980 income expressed in 1991 dollars}$$

The 1980 income is increased by the ratio of the 1991 price index to the 1980 price index: the $20,000 of income in 1980 is equivalent to $33,058 of income in 1991.

Here is another example. Your department used to present a $50 gift certificate to an outstanding employee. The last time this was done was in 1975. What would be a comparable award as of 1991?

To calculate the amount, you would multiply the $50 times the ratio of the 1991 value of the Consumer Price Index to the 1975 value:

$$50 \times \frac{\text{Average CPI value for 1991}}{\text{Average CPI value for 1975}}$$

$$= 50 \times \frac{136.2}{53.8} = 126.6$$

Consequently, you would probably want to make the gift certificate close to this amount, perhaps $125. (You can update this example by substituting in the appropriate CPI value.)

Where to Get Information on the Consumer Price Index

The Consumer Price Index is prepared monthly by the Bureau of Labor Statistics at the U.S. Department of Labor. The latest summary figures are available via a recorded message.[7]

Printed sources for the data include the *Monthly Labor Review* and the *CPI Detailed Report,* both published by the U.S. Department of Labor, and the *Survey of Current Business,* published by the U.S. Department of Commerce. These publications are available in many libraries. (Please see the appendix for listings.) I recommend that you use a government report of some type for your source, so that you can be sure you are using exactly the same index from month to month.

Summary

The Consumer Price Index shows change through time that has occurred, on average, in the prices of a set "market basket" of goods and services bought by urban households in the U.S. There is a CPI for "all urban consumers" and also for "urban wage earners and clerical workers." The "all urban" index represents a greater portion of the U.S. population.

The index is calculated relative to a base period. By taking the percentage change in the index values, you can assess price trends over a given period of time. The U.S. Bureau of Labor Statistics reports monthly changes in the CPI before and after adjustment for seasonal variations. Price indexes such as the CPI also provide a convenient way to take out the effects of price level changes on income or other economic measures, so that you can discern the "real" trends.

Notes

1. U.S. Department of Labor, Bureau of Labor Statistics, *Monthly Labor Review*, August 1990, p. 57. However, the composition of the market basket of goods and services is updated from time to time; the CPI was revised as of the release of January 1987 data and was previously revised in 1978.

2. Some components of the Consumer Price Index have a different base.

3. U.S. Department of Labor, Bureau of Labor Statistics, "BLS Update," Spring/Summer 1988, p. 1.

4. The base period was 1967 for most of the CPI indexes. "BLS Update," Spring/Summer 1988, p. 1.

5. U.S. Department of Labor, Bureau of Labor Statistics, "Using the Consumer Price Index for Escalation," Report 761, January 1989, p. 3.

6. U.S. Department of Labor, Bureau of Labor Statistics, *Handbook of Labor Statistics*, August 1989, p. 475. The following section of the text discusses price level adjustments during periods of inflation. The CPI can also be used to adjust for price level changes during periods of deflation.

7. The Bureau of Labor Statistics publishes a news release on the Consumer Price Index; data are also available electronically. As of the time of this writing, a recorded message on the "Consumer Price Index Hotline" and other current Bureau of Labor Statistics data can be reached via the information number at (202) 606-STAT (a toll call if you are phoning long distance).

Chapter Four

Inflation and Your Business: Part Two

Indexes are available for many types of prices. This chapter provides some details on the Consumer Price Index, following the discussion in Chapter Three, and presents some other important measures of price changes over time.

The Consumer Price Index: A Closer Look

The Consumer Price Index has component indexes for food and beverages, housing, apparel and upkeep, transportation, medical care, entertainment, and other goods and services, such as personal care. Information on these groupings appears in publications such as the *Monthly Labor Review*. These categories, in turn, are broken down into greater detail. Within food and beverages, for example, you will find listings for food, including food at home, under which are items such as dairy products or fruits and vegetables. There are also listings for food away from home and for alcoholic beverages.

If you need more specific information, you can turn to the *CPI Detailed Report,* which is also produced by the U.S. Department of Labor, Bureau of Labor Statistics. Here, under dairy products, for example, you will find specific items like fresh whole milk. Other particular items in the *CPI Detailed Report* include sirloin steak, coffee, telephone service (local, interstate and intrastate calls), sofas, postage, watches, new motorcycles, prescription drugs, and newspapers. In other words, there is information for a wide variety of goods and services.

The Consumer Price Index is a measure of relative, not absolute, prices over a period of months or years. The CPI allows you to analyze *trends* in the price of a given item or category *over a span of time.*

Why would you need such detailed pricing information? First, for competitive purposes, you would want to know about price changes in your product market. The 1991 annual average CPI (All Urban Consumers) for televisions was 72.9; since the index base is 1982-84 ($=100$), you know that the prices of televisions were about 27 percent less in 1991 than during 1982-84.[1]

If you produce greeting cards, you might be concerned about postage prices. The CPI (All Urban Consumers) for postage was 143.6 as of the 1991 annual average, indicating a 44 percent increase in price since 1982-84. Conversely, the annual average price index of interstate toll telephone calls stood at 67.6 in 1991, indicating a 32 percent decrease since the base period.[2] Thus, the relative attractiveness of long-distance calling may have grown—at least from a pricing standpoint—over this time period.

Detailed information can also help you understand the needs of your customers. If you deal with senior citizens, for example, you would want to be sensitive to price trends in medical care and utility services. For families with children at home, you would want to be aware of price trends in food, home ownership, clothing, and college tuition.

Price trends can also help in analyzing business decisions. If you have to evaluate employee benefit costs for your company, you might want to see how the prices of medical care have increased over time. The components of medical care include commodities (such as drugs) and services. Medical services include both professional services and hospital and related services.

If you are evaluating a van pool for your office, you might want to see what the price trends have been for private transportation: the changes in the prices of cars, fuel, maintenance, and repair.

Table 4.1 provides annual data from the Consumer Price Index for some representative categories. The transportation category in the table includes both private and public transportation. By taking the percentage changes in any category, you can see price trends in that particular area over time. You can compare the percentage change over time, for example, in food versus transportation or medical care.

Table 4.1
The Consumer Price Index, Selected Components
All Urban Consumers, U. S. City Average
Annual Averages (1982-84 = 100)

Year	Food	Shelter	Apparel and Upkeep	Trans-porta-tion	Medical Care
1970	39.2	35.5	59.2	37.5	34.0
1971	40.4	37.0	61.1	39.5	36.1
1972	42.1	38.7	62.3	39.9	37.3
1973	48.2	40.5	64.6	41.2	38.8
1974	55.1	44.4	69.4	45.8	42.4
1975	59.8	48.8	72.5	50.1	47.5
1976	61.6	51.5	75.2	55.1	52.0
1977	65.5	54.9	78.6	59.0	57.0
1978	72.0	60.5	81.4	61.7	61.8
1979	79.9	68.9	84.9	70.5	67.5
1980	86.8	81.0	90.9	83.1	74.9

Note: "Food" and "alcoholic beverages" are classified under the heading "food and beverages"; "shelter," along with "fuel and other utilities" and "household furnishings and operations," is under "housing."

Table 4.1 (continued)

Year	Food	Shelter	Apparel and Upkeep	Trans-porta-tion	Medical Care
1981	93.6	90.5	95.3	93.2	82.9
1982	97.4	96.9	97.8	97.0	92.5
1983	99.4	99.1	100.2	99.3	100.6
1984	103.2	104.0	102.1	103.7	106.8
1985	105.6	109.8	105.0	106.4	113.5
1986	109.0	115.8	105.9	102.3	122.0
1987	113.5	121.3	110.6	105.4	130.1
1988	118.2	127.1	115.4	108.7	138.6
1989	125.1	132.8	118.6	114.1	149.3
1990	132.4	140.0	124.1	120.5	162.8
1991	136.3	146.3	128.7	123.8	177.0

Source: U.S. Bureau of Labor Statistics, *Monthly Labor Review* and *Handbook of Labor Statistics*, in U.S. Bureau of the Census, *Statistical Abstract of the United States: 1990* (110th edition), Washington, D.C., 1990, p. 471; and *Monthly Labor Review*, August 1990, p. 83; March 1992, p. 75.

Producer Price Indexes

The U.S. Bureau of Labor Statistics, which prepares the Consumer Price Index, also computes Producer Price Indexes (formerly Wholesale Price Indexes). "Producer Price Indexes (PPI) measure average changes in prices received by domestic producers of commodities in all stages of processing."[3] A detailed listing of these indexes is available on a monthly basis in the *Producer Price Indexes* journal, published by the U.S. Department of Labor, Bureau of Labor Statistics.

The Producer Price Index covers price trends of thousands of commodities. The following list gives you an idea of the broad commodity categories:

Farm products
Processed foods and feeds
Textile products and apparel
Hides, skins, leather, and related products
Fuels and related products and power
Chemicals and allied products
Rubber and plastic products
Lumber and wood products
Pulp, paper, and allied products
Metals and metal products
Machinery and equipment
Furniture and household durables
Nonmetallic mineral products
Transportation equipment
Miscellaneous products

There are numerous divisions within each category. Under metals and metal products (commodity code 10), for example, there are divisions for iron and steel (code 101), nonferrous metals (code 102), metal containers (code 103), hardware (code 104), plumbing fixtures and brass fittings (code 105), heating equipment (code 106), fabricated structural metal products (code 107), miscellaneous metal products (code 108) and metal treatment services (code 109). Under hardware (code 104), we find two divisions: "hardware, not elsewhere classified" (code 1041) and "hand and edge tools" (code 1042). Under the second heading, there are items such as screwdrivers (code 1042 0141) and pliers (code 1042 0151).

Producer Price Indexes is a comprehensive source for Producer Price Index data. Publications such as the *Survey of Current Business* also have data for some Producer Price Indexes.

Producer Price Indexes are organized in three major ways. In addition to commodity indexes, there are indexes by "stage of processing," from crude to intermediate materials to finished goods. A third classification system is by industry, based on the Standard Industrial Classification (SIC) system (discussed in Chapter One) and related Census product codes.[4]

As with the Consumer Price Index, price changes are typically calculated as percentage changes. The base year of 1982 (equals 100) is used for many Producer Price Indexes, but other bases are also used.

Besides being used in contracts, as discussed in the following section, Producer Price Indexes are handy in analyzing the prices of commodities—such as inventories—over time. If the value of your inventories has increased, for example, the gain may be attributable to either price or quantity changes. If you know what the national escalation in certain prices has been, you can determine whether the price increases you have paid have been above or below national trends and whether the increased value of your inventories is attributable to inflation at all or to some other factor.

Price Indexes and Contracts

Contracts frequently have clauses that allow for adjustment of prices according to the change that occurs in a specified index. For example, a rental or lease agreement may include an adjustment for inflation as measured by the Consumer Price Index. The Bureau of Labor Statistics has a report entitled "Using the Consumer Price Index for Escalation," which you might want to read if you plan to use the CPI in contracts.[5]

A construction contract may include adjustments for the change in the cost of materials, such as lumber, cement, and pipe. If you intend to use Producer Price Indexes in contracts for price escalation, I would suggest that you read the Bureau of Labor Statistics publication, "Escalation and Producer Price Indexes: A Guide for Contracting Parties." This report explains a number of important items in applying Producer Price Indexes (PPI) to escalation agreements. For example, the PPI data are, as a matter of course, "subject to revision" four months after first publication,[6] and, therefore, if PPI data are used, the guidelines recommend that a contract indicate when price modifications will be calculated, using the most recent data available for a particular month (or, at a minimum, whether indexes will be used in their initially published or "final" form for a given month).[7]

Another issue you may want to consider in contract negotiations is that the particular escalation components on which you have agreed may increase significantly over time, but the market (as opposed to the contract) price of the final product may not, due to competition or changes in other factors. If you are a purchaser, you might pay more under a contract than if you had bought at the prevailing price at a later time. (Of course, you may also pay less under such a contract.)

Be aware that price escalators may not reflect all the factors that determine market values. As an extreme example, imagine that you had a contract to purchase a home in two years, with price adjustments for the cost of building materials. If during that two-year period, the real estate market in your area were to deteriorate, you would be able to purchase a similar home for a lower price. The contracted price, however, may have risen if there were significant increases in the price of building materials (whose prices were related to national rather than local conditions).

If instead there were a boom in your area, then your contract price could be a fine deal. Just remember that the other possibility exists, too.

Additional Price Indexes

In addition to the Consumer Price Index and the Producer Price Index, the U.S. government prepares broad-based measures of inflation related to the nation's gross domestic product. Previously, the Bureau of Economic Analysis, U.S. Department of Commerce, focused on the price index for gross national product as an overall inflation measure. Along with the shift in attention from gross national product to gross domestic product (as discussed in Chapter One), the emphasis is now on the price index for gross domestic product and the index for gross domestic purchases. The price index for gross domestic purchases tracks prices on purchases made by residents of the U.S. The index is based on the prices of personal consumption expenditures, gross private domestic investment, and government purchases.[8]

The statistics for gross domestic purchases are part of the extensive data that the Bureau of Economic Analysis publishes in the "national income and product accounts." Many price indexes are included in these accounts. For example, there are indexes for categories of national defense purchases, such as military aircraft, missiles, and ships. The base year for these index numbers is currently 1987.[9]

The Bureau of Economic Analysis publishes several types of price indexes. For example, fixed-weighted price indexes use constant weights from a base period for their components and thus measure price changes over time. By comparison, shifts in the makeup of GDP (or GNP) as well as price movements are captured in the Implicit Price Deflators.[10] Like the GDP (and GNP) figures, these price measures are subject to revision.

The indexes discussed thus far relate to price changes on a national level. Some regional statistics are also available. The U.S. Department of Labor, Bureau of Labor Statistics, publishes Consumer Price Index data for a number of areas, such as San Francisco-Oakland-San Jose, California; Cleveland-Akron-Lorain, Ohio; and Miami-Fort Lauderdale, Florida. The data allow you to analyze price trends over time for an area. These indexes, however, do not permit comparisons of living costs among communities at a given point in time.[11]

Data on living costs in different areas can be helpful when considering moves (and the associated compensation required for maintaining a standard of living). This information is collected by some organizations. The ACCRA Cost of Living Index makes such data available for a large number of places in the U.S. ACCRA's quarterly report presents indexes that allow comparisons of after-tax costs of living and components such as housing costs for a "midmanagement" living standard. Some ACCRA data have been reproduced by the U.S. Bureau of the Census in the *Statistical Abstract of the United States*.[12]

For public utilities, the firm of Whitman, Requardt and Associates publishes detailed information on trends of construction and material and labor costs, known as "Handy-Whitman Indexes." Indexes for specific categories of transmission, distribution, and generation costs are available for electric utilities, for example, and these are compiled semi-annually for major regions of the U.S.[13]

Using Price Indexes to Analyze Business Data

Let us consider an example using price indexes in a business situation. Suppose you have been asked to determine whether your department has become more efficient over time. The data that you were able to gather pertaining to departmental costs and the number of customers served between 1981 and 1991 are shown in Table 4.2.

Departmental costs increased by more than three times between 1981 and 1991. The number of customers tripled

Table 4.2
An Example of Average Cost Trends

Year	Department Costs ($)	Number of Customers	Average Cost per Customer ($)
1981	65,000	12	5,417
1982	80,000	14	5,714
1983	100,000	17	5,882
1984	120,000	20	6,000
1985	135,000	22	6,136
1986	155,000	25	6,200
1987	165,000	26	6,346
1988	180,000	28	6,429
1989	195,000	30	6,500
1990	225,000	34	6,618
1991	240,000	36	6,667

Table 4.3
An Example of Inflation-Adjusted Costs

Year	Dept. Costs ($)	CPI (1)	Inflation-Adjusted Costs (2)	No. of Customers	Inflation-Adjusted Costs per Customer ($)
1981	65,000	90.9	65,000 x 100/90.9 = 71,507	12	5,959
1982	80,000	96.5	80,000 x 100/96.5 = 82,902	14	5,922
1983	100,000	99.6	100,000 x 100/99.6 = 100,402	17	5,906
1984	120,000	103.9	120,000 x 100/103.9 = 115,496	20	5,775
1985	135,000	107.6	135,000 x 100/107.6 = 125,465	22	5,703
1986	155,000	109.6	155,000 x 100/109.6 = 141,423	25	5,657
1987	165,000	113.6	165,000 x 100/113.6 = 145,246	26	5,586

Table 4.3 (continued)

Year	Dept. Costs ($)	CPI (1)	Inflation- Adjusted Costs (2)	No. of Custom- ers	Inflation- Adjusted Costs per Customer ($)
1988	180,000	118.3	180,000 x 100/118.3 = 152,156	28	5,434
1989	195,000	124.0	195,000 x 100/124.0 = 157,258	30	5,242
1990	225,000	130.7	225,000 x 100/130.7 = 172,150	34	5,063
1991	240,000	136.2	240,000 x 100/136.2 = 176,211	36	4,895

[1]Consumer Price Index, All Urban Consumers, All Items, Annual Averages (1982-84 = 100). Source: U.S. Department of Labor, Bureau of Labor Statistics (see Table 3.2).

[2]In 1982-84 dollars.

over the period, and the average cost per customer rose by 23 percent. To what extent is the increase in the average cost attributable to inflation?

Table 4.3 applies inflation adjustments to the example described in Table 4.2. The Consumer Price Index data in the third column of Table 4.3 show inflation over the period. The fourth column presents the inflation-adjusted costs. All the costs are expressed in 1982-84 dollars, which means that the effects of inflation have been removed. The sixth (last) column shows that after adjustment for inflation, the department's costs per customer have actually decreased substantially. This result is consistent with the findings that per-customer costs have increased by 23 percent, less than the overall inflation of about 50 percent (136.2/90.9).

Consider still another example. Suppose your stock of stationery supplies in 1991 had an average value of $1,000. Your records show that, in 1985, stationery supplies had an average balance worth $700. Did the inventory balances increase proportionately to the rate of inflation?

Since your inventories have increased by 43 percent, the question is whether this is the same, less than, or more than, the rate of inflation. If we look at the Consumer Price Index over that period, we see that overall prices increased by 27 percent (136.2/107.6). Consequently, the growth in the inventory balance has surpassed the rate of general inflation. To focus this analysis more, you could look at the Producer Price Index for paper or for one of the writing paper categories.

Using price indexes to make inflation (or deflation) adjustments is a valuable way of analyzing underlying trends. It is an important first step to managing costs and to determining the reasons why expenditures have changed. There may also be changes in quantities or special price factors that need to be considered. Without a basic price trend analysis, however, you may incorrectly blame "inflation" in the overall economy for increases in expenses and not make the effort to control costs more effectively.

Summary

Consumer Price Index (CPI) data are available for various groupings, such as food and beverages or medical care. Data on price trends for detailed categories are also available. This type of information can assist you in analyzing price movements relative to your markets.

The Producer Price Indexes (PPI) provide another important perspective on price trends. Formerly known as "Wholesale Price Indexes," the PPI cover price changes for thousands of commodities. The U.S. Bureau of Labor Statistics has monthly releases on the CPI and PPI and publishes guides regarding the use of these indexes in contracts.

The Bureau of Economic Analysis in the U.S. Department of Commerce prepares numerous price indexes related to gross domestic product. These are published with the "national income and product accounts" and give you a broad perspective on price movements in the overall economy, as well as information related to various sectors, including business and government.

In addition to national price indexes, there are Consumer Price Indexes for various locations. Each of these area CPIs shows price changes over time for a specific place, not variations in the price level between places. The ACCRA Cost of Living Index provides information that allows comparisons of after-tax costs of living and of various component costs for a large number of places in the U.S.

Indexes can be helpful in analyzing data relevant to your business. Some available indexes relate to cost trends in specific industries, such as public utilities.

As discussed in Chapter Three, the CPI can be used to evaluate changes in income or other variables relative to inflation. Chapter Four shows how price indexes can help to reveal the underlying trend in indicators such as total costs or costs per customer. This type of analysis, in turn, may assist you in managing your business resources more effectively.

Notes

1. U.S. city average; U.S. Department of Labor, Bureau of Labor Statistics, *CPI Detailed Report,* January 1992, p. 162. In addition to the price indexes, the *CPI Detailed Report* includes certain data on average prices for energy (such as electricity per kilowatt-hour and gasoline per gallon) and for retail food (such as various types of meats or produce per pound). See, for example, *CPI Detailed Report, Data for July 1992*, Tables P1-P4.

2. All Urban Consumers, U.S. City Average; *Ibid.*, pp.161-62.

3. U.S. Department of Labor, Bureau of Labor Statistics, *Producer Price Indexes, Data for November 1991,* p. 202.

4. *Ibid.*

5. U.S. Department of Labor, Bureau of Labor Statistics, "Using the Consumer Price Index for Escalation," January 1989, Report 761. Bureau of Labor Statistics, Consumer Prices and Price Indexes, Washington, D.C. 20212.

6. U.S. Department of Labor, Bureau of Labor Statistics, "Escalation and Producer Price Indexes: A Guide for Contracting Parties," Report 807, September 1991, p. 3. U.S. Department of Labor, Bureau of Labor Statistics, Washington, D.C. 20212.

7. *Ibid.*, pp. 3-4. In addition to the regular revision schedule, note that PPI data are rebased from time to time. In a few cases, there may also be data corrections to PPI indexes. Therefore, it is important to be specific about the PPI version to be applied.

8. U.S. Department of Commerce, Bureau of Economic Analysis, *Survey of Current Business,* November 1991, p. 3; February 1992, pp. 7, 20. The price indexes for gross national product continue to be reported as well.

9. The base period for GNP previously was 1982. *Survey of Current Business,* February 1992, p. 23; November 1991, p. 1.

10. *Statistical Abstract of the United States*, 1990, p. 466. See the *Survey of Current Business* for these and other types of indexes.

11. U.S. Bureau of Labor Statistics, *Monthly Labor Review,* May 1992, p. 63. If the CPI is used in an escalation agreement, the BLS recommends that the U.S. City Average index be used rather than the indexes for local areas, due to their smaller samples ("Using the Consumer Price Index for Escalation," January 1989, p. 1).

12. ACCRA, 1992. In 1992, ACCRA changed its name from American Chamber of Commerce Researchers Association. To obtain subscription and ordering information, write to ACCRA, P.O. Box 6749, Louisville, Kentucky 40206-6749, or call the subscription office at 502-897-2890.

13. "The Handy-Whitman Index of Public Utility Construction Costs," Whitman, Requardt and Associates, 2315 Saint Paul Street, Baltimore, Maryland 21218.

Chapter Five

Economics and Your Financing

Financial decisions are part of running every business. Sometimes you need to make a choice as to the terms on which you will borrow money. At other times, you need to settle on terms at which to lend or invest money or to extend credit to customers.

In our economy, interest rates are determined by the supply of loanable funds and the demand for those funds. Our central bank, the Federal Reserve System, can influence the supply of funds. The demand for funds is determined by the borrowing activity of consumers, businesses, and government.

The Effects of Compounding

When you put money in a savings account, it earns interest, which is compounded over time. Thus, $100 invested today at 5 percent annual interest would grow to $105 at the end of a year:

$100 (1 + interest rate expressed as a decimal) =
$100 (1 + .05) = $105

At the end of two years, the amount would be

$100 (1.05) (1.05) = $110.25

During the second year, you will again earn $5 on the $100 plus you will earn 25 cents on the $5 you earned during the previous year.

Similarly, if you were going to be paid $110.25 at the end of two years, you would not be willing to invest more than $100 today, assuming a 5 percent rate of interest. The $100 represents the *present value* of the $110.25 to be received two years from now using a 5 percent *discount rate*.

$$ \$\$\$ \ \ \$\$\$ \ \ \$\$\$ \ \ \$\$\$ \ \ \$\$\$ $$

The concept of present value is a very useful tool for evaluating the worth today of money to be received at some future date. For example, consider the situation in which you were injured in an accident and were unable to earn your $30,000 salary for the next year. For simplicity, assume that you would have been paid the $30,000 in a lump sum at the end of the year. If you could earn 5 percent in a bank account, the present value of $30,000 (to be received at year-end) would be

$$\frac{\$30,000}{(1 + \text{interest rate expressed as a decimal})}$$

$$= \frac{\$30,000}{(1.05)} = \$28,571.43$$

In other words, about $28,571 in hand today is just as valuable as $30,000 a year from now, in an environment where the appropriate discount rate is 5 percent. The present values are the same. (We are excluding the impact of any other factors, such as taxes.)

Formulas for present values are built into many financial calculators and computer spreadsheet programs. You can easily find the present value of a stream of money over time. (Finance books will give you more information on calculating present values under a variety of circumstances.)

What interest rate should you choose in calculating present value? One approach is to pick the rate that is most representative of what you would earn if you had the money you are evaluating. Corporations often use interest rates that reflect their cost of obtaining funds through sales of stocks and bonds. Corporate or managerial finance books can provide you with information on calculating this type of rate or cost of capital. The higher the interest rate you pick, the lower will be the resulting present value, and the further into the future that the payoff occurs, the lower will be the present value.

Interest Rates and Inflation

We should also consider interest rates in the context of inflation. This introduces the concept of the "real interest rate" or the interest rate after an adjustment for inflation.[1] As you are well aware, the rate of inflation may sometimes be as great as the rate of interest your funds are earning, and, occasionally, may be even greater. To earn a positive "real" rate of interest, your funds must be invested at a rate higher than inflation. (Of course, what you project inflation to be may be different from what inflation actually turns out to be.)

Figure 5.1 offers a perspective on interest rates from the 1970s to the early 1990s. During about half the time for the

Figure 5.1
Selected Interest Rates, 1970-91

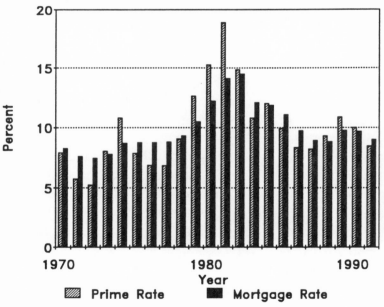

Note: Prime rate is on short-term loans from banks to business customers with the highest credit standing. Mortgage rate is for new homes (see source regarding data).
Source: U.S. Department of Commerce, Bureau of Economic Analysis, *Business Statistics, 1963-91* (Washington, D.C.: U.S. Government

Source (continued)
Printing Office, June 1992), p. 64. Bank prime rate is from the Board of
Governors of the Federal Reserve System. Home mortgage rate is from
the Office of Thrift Supervision for single-family homes, conventional
first mortgages, and is a "combined weighted average." For description
of data methodology, see *Business Statistics*, pp. 159-60 (notes for p. 64).
Home mortgage rates for 1989 and 1990 are "weighted by number of
loans." For current data, see the *Survey of Current Business*.

data shown, interest rates on short-term business loans (as
illustrated by the prime rate) were less than long-term home
mortgage rates. This is consistent with the proposition that
one is charged a higher rate on a loan to be repaid over a period
of many years as opposed to only a few months. Similarly,
we tend to expect to receive a higher return on a savings
certificate when we agree not to withdraw the funds for
several years as opposed to several weeks.

There were, however, almost as many occasions during
this time period when interest rates on short-term loans
exceeded long-term lending rates. This reversal in rates or
interest yields has sometimes occurred during periods of
relatively high inflation.

If you think inflation and interest rates will be lower in
the future, you, as a borrower, may prefer to take out a loan
on a short-term basis, with the hope of refinancing at a more
favorable rate later. Consequently, the demand for short-
term financing may result in an increase in rates on these loans
relative to rates on longer-term loans.

As you will note from Figure 5.2, higher rates of
inflation tend to be accompanied by higher interest rates. To
some extent, this reflects the natural tendency of lenders to
require higher interest rates to compensate for inflation.
Another factor is that during times of rapid inflation, the

Federal Reserve Board may act to restrain credit availability in the economy, resulting in higher interest rates.

There are also times when interest rates appear relatively high, yet inflation rates are moderate. Such comparatively high real rates of interest reflect the demand for and supply of funds, Federal Reserve policy, and expectations about inflation and the economy.

Figure 5.2

Interest Rates and Inflation, 1970-91

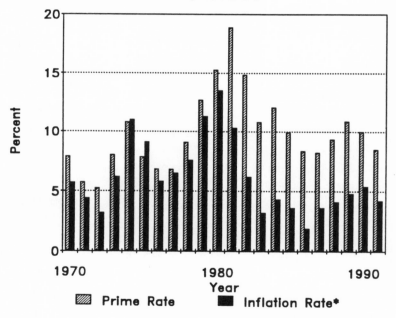

*Percent change based on annual averages, Consumer Price Index, All Urban Consumers. See Table 3.2 for methodology.
Source: See Tables 3.2 and 5.1.

Figures 5.1 and 5.2 show that interest rates have been substantial in recent history and thus can be a major budget item for businesses as well as for consumers. In addition, changes in interest rates may mean a significant difference in payments over time. Lower interest rates in 1992, for example, spurred a flurry of refinancing activity.

For a perspective on interest rate trends, review the data published in the monthly *Survey of Current Business.* For very recent data, look in *The Wall Street Journal,* which is published on weekdays.

Economics and Financing Costs

You can use economics to help lower your financing costs. The stronger your sales, the more you will be able to finance your expenditures from your own earnings. Less dependence on outside financing means lower total financing costs and can help you to get better rates on the funds you do borrow.

First, knowing the economic characteristics of your market will help you pick those areas that are most robust and have been least susceptible to downturns. In addition, you will want to cultivate a variety of types of customers. In other words, you do not want your business to be too dependent on a single source of revenues (or on customers whose fortunes rise and fall in unison.) See the "Economics and Planning" section of Chapter Seven for a further discussion of this topic.

Second, careful presentation of the economics of your market will reassure your creditors of the quality of their investment in your business. You should show investors what amounts to an economic album.

For each geographical area in which you operate, you should present clear pictures of population, employment, and the unemployment rate. You also need to describe personal income, retail sales, building permits, real estate vacancy rates, and other indicators pertinent to the market.

See Chapters One and Two for economic sources of information about your markets. The data should show trends over time and comparisons with national averages, where appropriate. Trying to secure the best financial terms is a type of marketing—and one in which economics is key.

Summary

Financial decisions have many dimensions, involving the valuation of money with respect to factors such as time, interest rates, and inflation. The concepts of compound interest and present value relate to the time dimension, while the real interest rate addresses the issue of financial returns relative to inflation.

Both supply and demand factors influence interest rates in our economy. Expectations by businesses and consumers about the economy and about inflation are other considerations that affect the profile of interest rates.

With regard to borrowing by individuals and organizations, lenders of funds are additionally concerned about the security of their investments. Consequently, the economic strength of your markets plays a crucial role in your obtaining financing at favorable terms.

Note

1. The topic of real interest rates has generated much discussion and actually has extensive historical roots. Thomas MacGillivray Humphrey analyzes the views of scholars Irving Fisher, Henry Thornton, and Alfred Marshall on monetary policy and real interest rates in "Can the Central Bank Peg Real Interest Rates? A Survey of Classical and Neoclassical Opinion," in Federal Reserve Bank of Richmond, *Economic Review,* September/October 1983, pp. 12-21. Discussions of real versus nominal interest rate concepts date back to the 1700s, as documented by Humphrey in "The Early History of the Real/Nominal Interest Rate Relationship," Federal Reserve Bank of Richmond, *Economic Review,* May/June 1983, pp. 2-10.

Chapter Six

Forecasts and Your Business

Most of us think about or make predictions in our daily lives. We listen to weather forecasts; we worry about next month's expenses; and we anticipate who will win elections to public office. Because of the day-to-day concerns that absorb much of our energy, we often focus on relatively short-term horizons. In business, this may cause us to ignore factors determining our longer-term ability to meet customers' needs and our own financial requirements.

Assessing the Future

Planning requires making assumptions about the future. Anticipated revenues and expenses are based on economics: the size and growth of the market, competition, and costs.

Economic forecasts are available to assist you in business planning. A number of firms specialize in producing economic predictions. Some companies concentrate on forecasts of the U.S. economy as a whole; others include forecasts of industries, geographic regions, and prices by specific categories, commodities, and services. Individual consultants also offer such information.

How good are predictions for the national economy? A few years ago, Stephen K. McNees, Vice President and Economist at the Federal Reserve Bank of Boston, published research that evaluated economic forecasts over lengthy periods of time: 35 years of annual forecasts and 12 years of quarterly forecasts. His research indicates that economic knowledge does contribute to the accuracy of forecasts of major factors such as overall growth in the economy and inflation. Most of the economic forecasts were produced using models combining economic and statistical formulas.[1]

It is sometimes hard to visualize an economic "model." A model represents the economy through a set of equations and may be very simple or extremely complex. A model of your income, for example, might consist of the following set of equations:

Income = Salary + Interest from bank accounts

where your Salary = (Your weekly wage)
times
(Number of weeks worked)

and

Interest from bank accounts =
(Amount of savings)
times
(The interest rate).

First, the model needs to express the relationship between components correctly. In the preceding example, you might have additional sources of income, such as stock dividends, which need to be included.

Second, to make a forecast, you will need to make certain assumptions. In the example that has been described, you would need to make assumptions about the interest rate you would be receiving on your savings.

Should your forecasts be optimistic or pessimistic? Being overly optimistic can cause you to ignore possible financial problems. Excessive pessimism can lead you to miss opportunities to expand your markets and to upgrade your products and services. Consequently, aim for the most realistic appraisal of the future and have every element of your forecast tied to the same underlying assumptions.

In addition, look at the impact of an unfavorable situation on your most important market and cost factors. Consider also what a strong increase in demand in your major markets would mean. This will give you boundaries within which you can expect to operate. Comparing your forecasts with your actual results can help you to pinpoint which factors were unexpected or need to be managed differently.

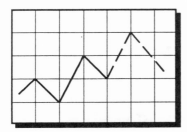 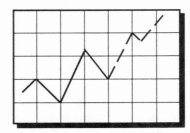

Although economic forecasting services can be extremely helpful, you do not have to subscribe to a service to obtain valuable insights on current trends and expected future developments. The U.S. Department of Commerce and U.S. Department of Labor are important sources of economic forecasts. Here are some examples.

Population

The U.S. Bureau of the Census (of the Department of Commerce) develops population forecasts for the nation. The predictions are based on suppositions about births, deaths, and net immigration (immigration to the U.S. less out-migration). The Census Bureau publishes extensive population projections. In Current Population Reports, Series P-25, for example, you can find long-term forecasts by age, race, and gender. The forecasts are very specific: as an illustration, you can find the projected number of white females who will be 41 years old in the year 2000.[2]

The Census Bureau also develops different sets of projections based on changes in the underlying assumptions about births, deaths, and net immigration. This allows you to assess the impacts that differences in these key demo-graphic variables might have. For example, if your company produces video games, you might want to know the projected size of the teenage population under assumptions of low, middle, or high births and under various immigration assumptions.[3]

Population trends determine the potential of your market. Analysis of population projections can give overall direction as to where to focus your development of products and services. Within a population segment, additional data—geographic, ethnic, gender—can help to identify more specific target groups. There are also Census Bureau predictions for the population of each state, by age and other characteristics.[4]

Employment

The U.S. Department of Labor, Bureau of Labor Statistics, develops extensive analyses of U.S. employment. Predictions are prepared for key variables such as the labor force, output and jobs by industry, and types of occupations. These projections, into the next century, are published in the *Monthly Labor Review.*[5]

The Bureau of Labor Statistics provides predictions for the labor force, categorized by gender, age, race and Hispanic origin. The Bureau also publishes economic forecasts and projections of output and employment by industry.

The outlook articles in the *Monthly Labor Review,* which are updated periodically, are a storehouse of information. The alternative forecasts provide a valuable range of estimates under high, moderate, and low growth situations.

The Bureau of Labor Statistics' predictions include data for a wide range of industries. Employment and output growth trends are predicted for manufacturing of goods as diverse as bakery products and aircraft and for services as different as advertising and beauty and barber shops.[6]

The Bureau of Labor Statistics also publishes predictions of jobs by occupation, in categories relating to executive, professional, technical, administrative, and other functions. These occupational categories are projected in considerable detail. To illustrate, the "engineers" group is broken down into categories including aeronautical/astronautical, chemical, civil, electrical/electronic, industrial, and mechanical.[7]

These and other types of occupational projections can give you background in serving your markets. For example, if you publish a magazine directed at dental hygienists, you might want to see employment forecasts for this occupation. The projections cover a wide variety of jobs, such as actuaries, landscape architects, meteorologists, and teachers.[8]

Regional Economics

The Bureau of Economic Analysis in the U.S. Department of Commerce prepares regional forecasts for several key indicators. You can obtain reports, for example, on states and metropolitan areas through the year 2040.[9] There are also forecast articles published in the *Survey of Current Business*. Projections show employment, inflation-adjusted earnings, and population for each state and region. In addition, employment and earnings data are shown for each state and region by major industry, such as mining, construction, manufacturing, and retail trade. In this way, you can compare the differing rates of growth forecasted for various areas.[10] You can also find projections for metropolitan statistical areas on population, employment, and income.[11]

Industries

The International Trade Administration of the U.S. Department of Commerce publishes the *U.S. Industrial Outlook* annually. This report is an outstanding source of information on many industries. Both manufacturing and services are covered. The industries include fields such as mining, construction, wood, building materials, textiles, paper products, chemicals, metals, plastic and rubber products, machinery, and electronics. Communication and information equipment and services are covered, as well as numerous consumer products. Travel, health, financial, publishing, and business services are also discussed in considerable detail.

The *U.S. Industrial Outlook* provides a wealth of information, with in-depth studies that include both historical background and market analysis. The discussions look at factors such as legislation, environmental concerns, employment, technology, costs, competition, taxation, demand, and opportunities. The report presents the prognosis for the current year and future trends.

The *U.S. Industrial Outlook* also gives perspective on business in an international context. It includes data on imports and exports and discusses key factors that affect the ability of U.S. companies to compete globally: economic trends, language considerations, and international trade settlements.

Other Forecasts

What about near-term forecasts of more immediate concerns, such as interest rates? Business magazines are a good source of near-term predictions. Often, projections appear in the fall and winter for the new year. *The Wall Street Journal* also publishes surveys of economists' forecasts.[12]

There are numerous statistical series that signal changes in the economy. The Business Cycle Indicators Branch, Bureau of Economic Analysis, U.S. Department of Commerce, compiles data on these major business barometers. The *Survey of Current Business* has a monthly data section on "Business Cycle Indicators." This shows various key indicators compiled by federal and other organizations, including several indexes that track attitudes of consumers.[13]

The composite index of leading indicators, a popular barometer of the business cycle, is a compilation of statistical data series that aid in forecasting business cycle highs and lows. The components of the index are based on various segments of the economy, such as construction (building permits for new private housing units) and manufacturing (including average weekly hours of nonsupervisory or production workers in manufacturing).[14]

If your markets are local or concentrated in specific areas, you may benefit from state economic sources. Numerous states have agencies that provide population and employment projections. Forecasts may also be available through the business schools of state universities, many of which have research centers that publish reports on regional economies.

Summary

Making assumptions about the future is central to business planning. "Models," through equations that represent relationships in the economy, provide one way of developing forecasts. In addition to private forecasting services, government agencies formulate predictions important to business; these include projections of population, employment, regional trends, and industry growth. Indicators that signal transitions in the business cycle are also available from government, as well as other, sources.

Notes

1. Stephen K. McNees, "How Accurate are Macroeconomic Forecasts?" *New England Economic Review* (Federal Reserve Bank of Boston), July/August 1988, p. 26.

2. U.S. Department of Commerce, Bureau of the Census, Current Population Reports, Series P-25, No. 1018, *Projections of the Population of the United States, by Age, Sex, and Race: 1988 to 2080,* by Gregory Spencer (Washington, D.C.: U.S. Government Printing Office, 1989), and, more recently, P25-1092, *Population Projections of the United States, by Age, Sex, Race, and Hispanic Origin: 1992 to 2050,* by Jennifer Cheeseman Day (Washington, D.C.: U.S. Government Printing Office, 1992).

3. *Ibid.*

4. U.S. Bureau of the Census, *Statistical Abstract of the United States: 1991,* 111th edition (Washington, D.C.: 1991), pp. 25-26. More detailed information can be found in Current Population Reports, "Population Estimates and Projections," Series P-25.

5. Projections through the year 2005 have been published in the *Monthly Labor Review* of November 1991. Previous projections, through the year 2000, were published in November 1989. Ronald E. Kutscher, "New BLS Projections: Findings and Implications," *Monthly Labor Review,* November 1991, pp. 3-12.

6. Max L. Carey and James C. Franklin, "Industry Output and Job Growth Continues Slow into Next Century," *Monthly Labor Review*, November 1991, pp. 45-63.

7. George Silvestri and John Lukasiewicz, "Occupational Employment Projections," *Monthly Labor Review*, November 1991, pp. 64-94; p. 68 lists these categories.

8. *Ibid.*, pp. 69-70.

9. "User's Guide to BEA Information," *Survey of Current Business*, February 1992, pp. 50-51.

10. Kenneth P. Johnson, John R. Kort, and Howard L. Friedenberg, "Regional and State Projections of Income, Employment, and Population to the Year 2000," *Survey of Current Business*, May 1990, pp. 33-54.

11. Regional Economic Analysis Division, "Metropolitan Statistical Area Projections of Income, Employment, and Population to the Year 2000," *Survey of Current Business*, October 1990, pp. 26-30.

12. For example, survey articles were published on July 6, 1992, and on January 4, 1993, based on end-of-year and mid-year polls. The articles were written by Tom Herman.

13. The sources for the consumer attitude indexes are the Survey Research Center, University of Michigan, and The Conference Board. See, for example, *Survey of Current Business*, October 1992, p. C-4 and accompanying note.

14. *Survey of Current Business*, February 1992, p. C-1, and Marie P. Hertzberg and Barry A. Beckman, "Business Cycle Indicators: Revised Composite Indexes," *Survey of Current Business*, January 1989, pp. 23-28.

Chapter Seven

Economics and Your Business Management

In our roles as consumers and members of households, our financial goals may be very simple: pay our bills and earn a decent living. To run a business, you also need to set financial objectives. Economics can contribute to setting goals that will help us to make the most of our resources and to face competition as effectively as possible.

In economic terms, becoming more productive means achieving greater output with the same inputs or realizing the same level of output with fewer inputs. In other words, the ratio of output to input is improving. You can set productivity goals for your business. If you expect to manufacture and sell 10 percent more next year, a possible productivity goal would be to have your costs increase by less than 10 percent. This may be easily attainable for a manufacturing company with unused capacity; the same machinery could be used to produce greater quantities of output.

Productivity increases may be more difficult to achieve in a service business. Still, controlling costs is important. For example, you may want to limit your costs per customer or per unit of output over time. You will need to decide what a reasonable limit is, based on what you see as unavoidable cost increases and your assessment of competition in your industry.

Economics and Organizational Goals

Financial analysts are very conscious of indicators of a company's fiscal health. There are numerous financial ratios that are monitored closely, to check a firm's profitability and the extent to which it has sufficient cash to meet its obligations.

An organization should also watch how efficiently its basic economic resources are being used. What has been the record of labor costs over time and relative to national and local trends? These costs can be measured on a per-worker basis and compared with indicators like hourly earnings, available in publications such as the U.S. Department of Labor's *Employment and Earnings*. Movements in benefit costs should be tracked and compared with similar government data. The Consumer Price Index has a separate category for medical care, which gives you a perspective on your own organization's trends.

Table 7.1 shows data for the Employment Cost Index for private industry.[1] The U.S. Bureau of Labor Statistics compiles the ECI to show trends in labor costs experienced by employers. The index is a quarterly indicator of the rate of change in compensation per hour of work. It comprises

Table 7.1
Employment Cost Index, Private Industry*

Period	Compensation	Wages & Salaries	Benefits (Costs to Employers)
	Percent Change		
Dec. 1980-Dec. 1981	9.9	8.8	12.1
Dec. 1981-Dec. 1982	6.5	6.3	7.2
Dec. 1982-Dec. 1983	5.7	4.9	7.4
Dec. 1983-Dec. 1984	4.9	4.2	6.5
Dec. 1984-Dec. 1985	3.9	4.1	3.5
Dec. 1985-Dec. 1986	3.2	3.2	3.4
Dec. 1986-Dec. 1987	3.3	3.3	3.4
Dec. 1987-Dec. 1988	4.8	4.1	6.9
Dec. 1988-Dec. 1989	4.8	4.1	6.1
Dec. 1989-Dec. 1990	4.6	4.0	6.6
Dec. 1990-Dec. 1991	4.4	3.7	6.2

*Excludes household and farm workers.
Source: U.S. Department of Labor, Bureau of Labor Statistics, Division of Employment Cost Trends, "Employment Cost Index--Historical Data,"January 28, 1992, pp. 30, 63, 94, from tables of not seasonally adjusted data, and Bureau of Labor Statistics, *News,* "Employment Cost Index—December 1991," p.1. Current data are in the *Monthly Labor Review.*

wages and salaries and the employer costs of benefits to employees. The ECI shows change over time in the cost to employers of employing workers. The ECI is based on a fixed market basket of labor, resembling conceptually the fixed market basket of goods and services in the Consumer Price Index.[2]

As you can see in Table 7.1, in most recent years, the rate of increase in benefit costs has surpassed the rate of increase in wages and salaries. This trend is not surprising, given the dramatic price rises in areas like medical care. (See Table 4.1 for data on price trends in medical care.) For businesses that provide these benefits, this means significant increases in expenses.

In addition to total labor costs and costs per employee over time, you should consider your investment per employee, in space, equipment, and supplies, and output per employee. How can you make reasonable projections of your needs over time unless you know what your past experience has been?

National productivity information can give you some general perspectives. Table 7.2 shows data on output per hour in recent years. The data are in index form, with a base of 1982 = 100. As you can see, productivity, as measured by output per hour in the nonfarm business area, has fluctuated a bit from year to year, but the trend is generally upward. At the start of the 1990s, the index was about 8 percent above its 1982 level. Specific industries have

Table 7.2
Output per Hour
All Persons, Nonfarm Businesses

Year	Annual Index (1982 = 100)
1982	100.0
1983	102.4
1984	104.5
1985	105.4
1986	107.5
1987	108.3
1988	109.2
1989	108.2
1990	108.4
1991	109.1

Source: Division of Productivity Research, Office of Productivity and Technology, U.S. Department of Labor, Bureau of Labor Statistics, "Industry Analytical Ratios for the Nonfarm Business Sector, All Persons," March 10, 1992 for 1980-89. For 1990-91, *Monthly Labor Review*, August 1992, p. 106. Data are subject to revision.

their own productivity trends, but, in general, in order to stay competitive over time, your business needs to achieve greater output per hour of work by employees.

Analyzing Sales, Inflation, and Productivity

Let us say that you have a business with sales figures as shown in Table 7.3. Sales have grown in every year but 1982. Between 1981 and 1991, the overall gain was 90 percent. The number of employees has also grown, by 70 percent. We can then calculate that the dollar amount of sales per employee has increased over the period, from $52,000 in 1981 to $58,235 in 1991.

The dollar increase in total sales reflects two factors: quantity and price. To look at the impact of price increases on sales, we can adjust each year's sales figures by a price index. The data in Table 7.4 show the sales figures adjusted by the Consumer Price Index. To be more precise, you could use a specialized price index; if you were evaluating retail food sales, for example, you might use the CPI for food.

After adjustment for price changes, sales increased by about 27 percent between 1981 and 1991 (even with a decline in 1991). This means that if there had been no inflation over the time period, sales in 1991 would have been about 27 percent greater than in 1981.

Another way to measure sales increases independent of inflation would be to analyze changes in the quantity sold over time. A pharmacy could look at the number of prescriptions filled, for example. An electric utility could look at kilowatt-hours of energy sold. The difficulty arises when there is a mix of products or services. It is hard to add units like greeting

Table 7.3
An Example of Sales Trends per Employee

Year	Sales ($)	Number of Employees	Sales per Employee
1981	520,000	10	52,000
1982	515,000	10	51,500
1983	540,000	11	49,091
1984	580,000	11	52,727
1985	670,000	12	55,833
1986	750,000	13	57,692
1987	800,000	14	57,143
1988	850,000	15	56,667
1989	910,000	16	56,875
1990	975,000	17	57,353
1991	990,000	17	58,235
% Change 1981-91	90%	70%	12%

Table 7.4
An Example of Inflation-Adjusted Trends

Year	Sales ($)	CPI*	Inflation-Adjusted Sales	Employees	Inflation-Adjusted Sales per Employee
1981	520,000	90.9	572,057	10	57,206
1982	515,000	96.5	533,679	10	53,368
1983	540,000	99.6	542,169	11	49,288
1984	580,000	103.9	558,229	11	50,748
1985	670,000	107.6	622,677	12	51,890
1986	750,000	109.6	684,307	13	52,639
1987	800,000	113.6	704,225	14	50,302
1988	850,000	118.3	718,512	15	47,901
1989	910,000	124.0	733,871	16	45,867
1990	975,000	130.7	745,983	17	43,881
1991	990,000	136.2	726,872	17	42,757

*Consumer Price Index, All Urban Consumers, All Items (1982-84 = 100).
Source: CPI data, U.S. Department of Labor, Bureau of Labor Statistics (see Table 3.2).

cards, stationery, and novelties at a gift shop: the number of items would not be as important as the actual volume of sales. Taking the dollar total and then adjusting for inflation allow you to combine very different types of goods and services and to look at underlying trends.[3]

After adjustment for inflation, the sales figures in our example have not kept pace with the growth in employment. As shown above, inflation-adjusted sales per employee have actually fallen between 1981 and 1991. Thus, although total sales have increased over the ten-year period, productivity, as measured by inflation-adjusted sales per worker, has dropped.

Could this situation have been avoided? Between 1981 and 1986, the company saw a 44 percent increase in sales. By then, employment had climbed by 30 percent. After adjustment for inflation, sales had increased by only 20 percent. Thus, the 30 percent addition to personnel may not have been justified. Similarly, between 1986 and 1990, employment rose by 31 percent, while inflation-adjusted sales increased by only 9 percent.

It is true that sales growth was quite rapid in 1985 and 1986. Still, given the sales-to-employee ratios in the early 1980s, the company may well have been able to handle the workload without adding as many people. In situations such as these, a basic analysis of inflation and productivity trends helps to provide guidelines to manage resources more effectively.

Economics and Planning

As a planner or manager, you need to have a broad economic view of your business. If you deal with individuals or departments, you will likely have a limited perspective, based on their requirements for personnel, equipment, and space. In the aggregate, their total demands may far surpass levels justified or sustainable by future revenues.

Consequently, for your business as a whole to be more productive, you need to have an overview of your anticipated sales, based on expectations of quantities and prices that reflect competition. From that forecast, you can deduce staffing, space, and equipment guidelines. No one component has to be absolute, but the sum of the overall costs needs to balance out to fit within your projected requirements and spending limits.

Each of these components should have a relationship to your expected sales level and to historical trends, such as sales per employee over time. You also need to consider inflation adjustments. For example, if the prices you are charging are up by 5 percent, then sales per employee should be expected to increase by at least 5 percent (so that inflation-adjusted sales are stable or growing). You should build in some productivity adjustment, as improved skills and better equipment increase the potential from your available resources.

Planning horizons vary according to the type of business and the type of activity within that business. Some companies are easily affected by every change in the market, in competition or in costs. Such businesses need to be very responsive to current trends. Other organizations are able to weather many disturbances in the overall economy, but it is also difficult to make quick changes in these businesses when market conditions shift. For these companies, capital requirements tend to be very large, and the consequences of mistakes are also substantial. These firms need two sets of plans: one for immediate concerns and another directed towards longer-term issues.

Economic forecasts can help you in your planning efforts by pointing out general trends: faster or slower overall growth, higher or lower rates of inflation. Unfortunately, forecasts seldom predict the specific ups and downs of the economy, i.e., exactly when economic turning points for recessions and expansions will occur. Unless you are a speculator at heart, you do not want to base business decisions solely on the success of a forecast in predicting the precise timing of a business cycle—or on the exact magnitude of an economic indicator.

What about diversification? Chapter One presented the need for market balance as well as growth. Certainly, diversity in revenue sources is desirable, as it helps an organization weather downturns in a given market segment. How can an organization increase the diversity of its revenue base? First, you need to determine the degree of diversity of the existing base through analysis of sales data by major customer or product class. Then, it is essential to see how these sales look over time and especially how closely they move together. If all your sales categories show the same trends, and particularly if they have a record of decreasing simultaneously, your sales base needs greater diversity.

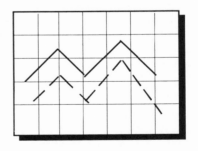

Does this mean that a computer company should sell cosmetics, since these are two markets that are unrelated? Probably not. Such economic diversification would not be expected to capitalize on special strengths and expertise. A successful singer can increase her diversity with a wider repertoire of songs. She doesn't have to become a mediocre violinist. Similarly, a business can increase its diversity by finding new applications for its products and by broadening its base of customers.

Economics and Your Business

Most of a company's major support needs are provided by accounting, finance, and marketing, with some ancillary functions such as insurance or law. These are the services essential to the smooth operation of a business. Economics is removed from many of these day-to-day concerns.

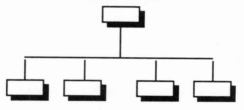

Economics, nevertheless, is central to your operations. Even a well-run company may have a bleak future if the demand for its product or service is declining. Economic statistics point out population and industry trends and make it possible to spot where growth is—and is not—occurring. Conversely, with inadequate control of costs, a company in a growth market may be bested by its competition. A simple comparison with inflation trends would help to determine if internal (i.e., management) or external factors are linked with increasing costs.

Economics gives you perspective—on your industry, your company, and your markets. With economic data, you can better analyze a situation over time, taking out the effects of inflation to evaluate the underlying movement. You can compare your own business earnings or costs with national trends. More sophisticated tools are also available, to help you determine mathematically the extent to which various factors are associated with final outcomes.[4] Economic analysis, for example, can indicate the degree to which consumer income or age or location may explain spending on a particular good or service.

The complexity of running a business today can be overwhelming. Yet, many decisions of enormous consequence boil down to very simple choices: increase or decrease the capacity of your plant, hire or lay off workers. Whether you have your own business or work for someone else, economics can help you to understand and develop markets, lower financing costs, and control operating expenses. Economic tools will help you do your job more effectively.

Here are a few key principles to keep in mind:

* **Think of economics as a process.** Look at trends over time and how indicators (such as your sales) are changing. Some people think of economics as a series of separate events—recessions or booms—and lose track of the gradual developments that signal major changes for a business.

* **Use economics as a competitive tool—not as an excuse.** Take out the effects of inflation to spot the underlying trend in sales or in inventory changes. Do not just assume that "inflation" is causing costs to increase. Inflation may not be the culprit at all or may be only one contributor to rising expenses.

91

* **Take time to understand the economic data that relate to your job and to the business in general.** Make sure that the particular data (or the time period) that you observe are truly representative. If someone presents cause-and-effect data to you, ask if there could be any other explanations for the conclusions.

* **Explore readily available sources of economic information.** There is a world of economic material available to you, and, in many cases, at minimal cost. Becoming familiar with a few top economic sources can be a powerful investment in your professional future.

Notes

1. ECI data are also available for state and local government and for the "civilian" sector, which is the sum of the private and the state and local government areas and omits household, farm, and federal government employment (U.S. Department of Labor, Bureau of Labor Statistics, Division of Employment Cost Trends, "Employment Cost Index--Historical Data," January 28, 1992, p. 7).

2. U.S. Department of Labor, Bureau of Labor Statistics, Compensation and Working Conditions.

3. This is a basic approach to adjusting for inflation. For more information about constructing price indexes, see, for example, Charles Mason and Clifford Butler, "New Basket of Goods and Services Being Priced in Revised CPI," *Monthly Labor Review*, January 1987, pp. 3-22, or the Bureau of Labor Statistics, *Handbook of Methods*.

4. Regression analysis is available in computer spreadsheet programs and on many financial calculators.

A Note to Nonprofit Organizations

As a not-for-profit organization, your institution likely has a clientele for which your services are essential. Competition, in the traditional sense, is not an issue. Frequently, your clients need too much rather than too little of your services.

Still, competition is a consideration for nonprofit organizations. The more efficiently you use your given resources, the greater the proportion of your funding goes to help your clients. Furthermore, individuals will be more apt to donate time and money to a well-run organization.

From the operations side, the staff of a nonprofit organization is just as sensitive to increases in living costs as employees of for-profit firms. Employees will still need to be compensated in keeping with market trends, allowing for some intangible benefits of working for your organization or cause and for possibly outstanding working conditions (perhaps flexible hours). In addition, your top performers will be the ones most likely to be attracted by higher wages elsewhere.

Unless your facilities, equipment, and materials are donated, you must also deal with cost increases in these areas. The chapters on inflation are important to consider in light of price increases imposed by your suppliers. You will also want to evaluate price changes that may be presented to you as being in line with the market.

Keeping track of economic trends is important. A slowing economy, one in which companies may be freezing staff levels or cutting jobs, poses a more difficult setting for fund raising than one in which businesses are hiring and unemployment rates are low. New businesses provide fresh potential sources of volunteers and funding for worthy causes, especially those with a civic focus that benefits the community and provides good public relations—and publicity—for the company.

Awareness of trends in your local economy and the markets served by local companies also helps you to relate to business people. Being able to understand the concerns of business can increase your credibility and help you to communicate your needs more effectively to the public.

Appendix

Resources

Chapter One

U.S. Department of Commerce. Bureau of Economic Analysis. *Survey of Current Business*. Monthly.

U.S. Department of Labor. Bureau of Labor Statistics. *Employment and Earnings*. Monthly.

_____. *Handbook of Labor Statistics*. Washington, D.C.: Superintendent of Documents, U.S. Government Printing Office.

Note: Check for the latest editions of the resources in this appendix.

Chapter Two

Board of Governors of the Federal Reserve System. *Federal Reserve Bulletin*. Monthly.

Executive Office of the President. Office of Management and Budget. *Standard Industrial Classification Manual*, 1987. Springfield, Va.: National Technical Information Service.

Federal Reserve Bank of Philadelphia. *The Fed in Print*. Federal Reserve Bank of Philadelphia, Research Department, 4th Floor, Publications Desk, 10 Independence Mall, Philadelphia, Pennsylvania 19106.

Federal Reserve System. District Federal Reserve Banks: Atlanta, Boston, Chicago, Cleveland, Dallas, Kansas City, Minneapolis, New York, Philadelphia, Richmond, St. Louis, San Francisco. (There are also branches and offices of the district banks in other cities.) The Board of Governors of the Federal Reserve System is located in Washington, D.C.

U.S. Congress. *Economic Report of the President*. Washington, D.C. : U.S. Government Printing Office.

U.S. Congress. Joint Economic Committee. *Economic Indicators*. Prepared by the Council of Economic Advisers. Washington, D.C.: U.S. Government Printing Office. Monthly.

U.S. Department of Commerce. Bureau of the Census. *County and City Data Book*. Washington, D.C.: U.S. Government Printing Office.

U.S. Department of Commerce. Bureau of the Census. Current Construction Reports, C40, *Housing Units Authorized by Building Permits*. Washington, D.C. : U.S. Government Printing Office. Monthly.

_____.*Guide to the Economic Censuses and Related Statistics*, EC 87-R-2. January 1990.

_____.*1987 Census of Manufactures*.

_____.*1990 Census of Population (1990 CP), 1990 Census of Housing (1990 CH), 1990 Census of Population and Housing (1990 CPH)*.

_____. *Statistical Abstract of the United States*. Washington, D.C.: Superintendent of Documents, U.S. Government Printing Office.

U.S. Department of Commerce. Bureau of the Census. Economics and Statistics Administration. *County Business Patterns*.

U.S. Department of Commerce. Bureau of Economic Analysis. *Survey of Current Business*. Monthly.

_____. "User's Guide to BEA Information." *Survey of Current Business*, February 1992, pp. 37-58.

U.S. Department of Labor. Bureau of Labor Statistics. *Employment and Earnings*. Monthly.

Chapter Three

Mason, Charles, and Clifford Butler. "New Basket of Goods and Services Being Priced in Revised CPI." *Monthly Labor Review*, January 1987, pp. 3-22.

U.S. Department of Commerce. Bureau of the Census. *Statistical Abstract of the United States*. Washington, D.C.: Superintendent of Documents, U.S. Government Printing Office.

U.S. Department of Commerce. Bureau of Economic Analysis. *Survey of Current Business*. Monthly.

U.S. Department of Labor. Bureau of Labor Statistics. "BLS Update." Spring/Summer 1988.

_____. *CPI Detailed Report*. Monthly.

_____. *Handbook of Labor Statistics*.

_____. *Monthly Labor Review*. Monthly.

_____. *News*. "The Consumer Price Index--January 1988."

_____. "Using the Consumer Price Index for Escalation." Report 761. January 1989.

Chapter Four

ACCRA Cost of Living Index. Subscription and ordering information: ACCRA, P.O. Box 6749, Louisville, Kentucky 40206-6749 (Subscription Office telephone: 502-897-2890).

"The Handy-Whitman Index of Public Utility Construction Costs." Whitman, Requardt and Associates, 2315 Saint Paul Street, Baltimore, Maryland 21218.

U.S. Department of Commerce, Bureau of the Census. *Statistical Abstract of the United States*. Washington, D.C.: Superintendent of Documents, U.S. Government Printing Office.

_____. Bureau of Economic Analysis. *Survey of Current Business*. Monthly.

U.S. Department of Labor. Bureau of Labor Statistics. *CPI Detailed Report*. Monthly.

_____. "Escalation and Producer Price Indexes: A Guide for Contracting Parties." Report 807. September 1991.

_____. *Monthly Labor Review*. Monthly.

_____. *Producer Price Indexes*. Monthly.

_____. "Using the Consumer Price Index for Escalation." Report 761. January 1989.

Chapter Five

Humphrey, Thomas MacGillivray. "Can the Central Bank Peg Real Interest Rates? A Survey of Classical and Neoclassical Opinion." Federal Reserve Bank of Richmond, *Economic Review*, September/October 1983, pp. 12-21.

_____. "The Early History of the Real/Nominal Interest Rate Relationship." Federal Reserve Bank of Richmond, *Economic Review*, May/June 1983, pp. 2-10.

U.S. Department of Commerce. Bureau of Economic Analysis. *Business Statistics, 1963-91*. Washington, D.C. : U.S. Government Printing Office, June 1992.

_____. *Survey of Current Business*. Monthly.

The Wall Street Journal. "Money & Investing" section.

Chapter Six

Carey, Max L., and James C. Franklin. "Industry Output and Job Growth Continues Slow into Next Century." *Monthly Labor Review*, November 1991, pp. 45-63.

Hertzberg, Marie P., and Barry A. Beckman. "Business Cycle Indicators: Revised Composite Indexes." *Survey of Current Business*, January 1989, pp. 23-28.

Johnson, Kenneth P., John R. Kort, and Howard L. Friedenberg. "Regional and State Projections of Income, Employment, and Population to the Year 2000." *Survey of Current Business*, May 1990, pp. 33-54.

Kutscher, Ronald E. "New BLS Projections: Findings and Implications." *Monthly Labor Review*, November 1991, pp. 3-12.

McNees, Stephen K. "How Accurate are Macroeconomic Forecasts?" *New England Economic Review* (Federal Reserve Bank of Boston), July/August 1988, pp. 15-36.

Silvestri, George, and John Lukasiewicz. "Occupational Employment Projections." *Monthly Labor Review*, November 1991, pp. 64-94.

U.S. Department of Commerce. Bureau of the Census. Current Population Reports, Series P-25, No. 1018. *Projections of the Population of the United States, by Age, Sex, and Race: 1988 to 2080*, by Gregory Spencer. Washington, D.C.: U.S. Government Printing Office, 1989.

_____. Current Population Reports. P25-1092. *Population Projections of the United States, by Age, Sex, Race, and Hispanic Origin: 1992 to 2050*, by Jennifer Cheeseman Day. Washington, D.C.: U.S. Government Printing Office, 1992.

U.S. Department of Commerce. Bureau of the Census. *Statistical Abstract of the United States*. Washington, D.C.: Superintendent of Documents, U.S. Government Printing Office.

U.S. Department of Commerce. Bureau of Economic Analysis. "User's Guide to BEA Information." *Survey of Current Business*, February 1992, pp. 37-58.

U.S. Department of Commerce. International Trade Administration. *U.S. Industrial Outlook.*

U.S. Department of Commerce. Regional Economic Analysis Division. "Metropolitan Statistical Area Projections of Income, Employment, and Population to the Year 2000." *Survey of Current Business*, October 1990, pp. 26-30.

Chapter Seven

U.S. Department of Labor. Bureau of Labor Statistics. *Monthly Labor Review.* Monthly.

U.S. Department of Labor. Bureau of Labor Statistics. Division of Employment Cost Trends. "Employment Cost Index--Historical Data," January 28, 1992.

U.S. Department of Labor. Bureau of Labor Statistics. Division of Productivity Research. Office of Productivity and Technology. "Industry Analytical Ratios for the Nonfarm Business Sector, All Persons," March 10, 1992.

Index

107

The Author

Business economist and writer Susan Krug Friedman has a B.A. degree in economics from Wellesley College, an M.A. in economics from Western Michigan University, and an M.B.A. from Arizona State University. She has had over fifteen years of on-the-job experience in applied economic research, analysis, and writing, including more than twelve years at a public utility. Susan Friedman has published articles on business and economic topics in professional journals and national magazines. Now based in Bloomington, Indiana, she is the author of *Notable Projects from Public Utilities: Innovations and Progressive Programs in Services, Marketing, and Resources/Operations from U.S. Electric (and Gas) Utilities.*